Literature Circles That Engage Middle and High School Students

Victor J. Moeller and Marc V. Moeller

EYE ON EDUCATION
6 DEPOT WAY WEST, SUITE 106
LARCHMONT, NY 10538
(914) 833–0551
(914) 833–0761 fax
www.eyeoneducation.com

Library of Congress Cataloging-in-Publication Data

Moeller, Victor J., 1937-
  Literature circles that engage middle and high school students / Victor J. Moeller and Marc V. Moeller.
     p. cm.
  Includes bibliographical references.
  ISBN 978-1-59667-062-4
1. Group reading--United States. 2. Book clubs (Discussion groups)--United States. 3. Literature--Study and teaching (Middle school)--United States. 4. Literature--Study and teaching (Secondary)--United States. 5. Student-centered learning--United States.
I. Moeller, Marc V., 1970- II. Title.
  LC6631.M64 2007
  428.4071'2--dc22

2007019395

10 9 8 7 6 5 4 3 2

Editorial and production services provided by
Hypertext Book and Journal Services
738 Saltillo St., San Antonio, TX 78207-6953 (210-227-6055)

Also Available from EYE ON EDUCATION

MEET THE AUTHORS

Victor J. Moeller has taught college rhetoric, English literature, American literature, and world literature in private and public high schools and colleges. He was an in-service field instructor for the Great Books Foundation, Chicago, IL for 14 years. In 1975, he became area director of professional development for Minnesota. During his years with the Chicago Foundation, he has conducted the Great Books Basic and Advanced Leader Training Course in 36 states. He has master degrees in English and education. Victor Moeller currently teaches at McHenry County College, Crystal Lake, Illinois, and may be reached at his Web site victormoeller.com or by e-mail at victormoeller@comcast.net. Since 2000, he has also been a reader of the Advanced Placement English Literature and Language Exam and consultant for the College Board. He has written several books on active learning, discussion, and the Socratic method: *English Teacher's Guide to Active Learning* (HS & MS), *Socratic Seminars and Literature Circles* (HS & MS), *Literature Circles That Engage Middle & High School Students*, *AP Great Book Seminars and Film: Ten Themes* (HS & College), *AP Shakespeare Seminars and Film: Five Tragedies & Five Comedies* and *College Rhetoric: What Every Student Should Know.*

Marc V. Moeller has taught courses in high schools and middle schools ranging from AP English (rhetoric and English literature) to English as a second language. His master's degree in education is from National Louis University of Chicago. He readily admits that the greatest influence on his teaching career has been Victor Moeller, his father and mentor. Marc Moeller currently teaches English at Prairie Middle School in Barrington, Illinois and may be reached by e-mail at marcanna@chicago.avenew.com.

ACKNOWLEDGMENTS

Harvey Daniels deserves enormous credit for developing and spreading litera-ture circles as a most effective method of getting kids hooked on books. We have relied largely on his two seminal books: *Literature Circles: Voice and Choice in the Stu-dent-Centered Classroom* (1994) and its sequel, *Literature Circles: Voice and Choice in Book Clubs and Reading Groups* (2002).

TABLE OF CONTENTS

PREFACE

"Learning is not a spectator sport."

♦ Teachers talk too much.

♦ Telling a student to think is like telling a student to fly.

♦ There can be no learning without discipline.

♦ The school that fails to teach thinking fails in everything.

♦ The student, not the teacher, is the primary agent of learning.

♦ Nothing is more daunting for a teacher than to get a student to think.

♦ Teaching is not chiefly about passing out information.

♦ The best kind of discipline is to engage students in engrossing activities.

♦ If thinking were easy, there would be more of it.

♦ The role of the teacher is to uncover the question that an answer hides.

♦ Thoughtful teachers create thoughtful students.

♦ Thinking is a skill that has to be practiced daily like playing the piano.

♦ Authentic learning begins when students are challenged with real questions—problems about meaning that demand solutions.

♦ Students asking students real questions leads to life-long learning.

Dear Colleague,

If you agree with most, or at least some of these statements, you have found kindred spirits. As we shake your hand and get a chair for you, let us explain briefly how this book will help you become a better teacher. Everything in this book is based on the assumption that students, not teachers, are the primary agents in learning. The corollary is that authentic learning is active learning. The consequence is that students become responsible for their own learning.

This book introduces you to a method—student-centered, collaborative learning—Literature Circles. Like their predecessor and complement, Great Book Groups, they have common, immediate goals of developing independent, reflective, and critical thinking and increasing student understanding and enjoyment of literature. Both methods also share the ultimate goal of enabling students to become life-long readers, and as a result, life-long learners.

The readings in this book are grouped around five themes or basic questions: (1) Who are your real friends? (DiCamillo, *Winn-Dixie*, and Neugeboren, "Luther"). (2) When do you need family most? (Updike, "Separating" and Hansberry, *A Raisin in the Sun*). (3) How important is a brother, a sister, or a girlfriend in your life? (Carson McCullers, "Sucker," Jean Stafford, "Bad Characters," William Faulkner, "Two Soldiers," and Leo Tolstoy, "Two Brothers." (4) How do true leaders inspire followers while false leaders deceive theirs? (Orwell, *Animal Farm* and C. S. Lewis, *The Lion, The Witch, and the Wardrobe*), and (5) Is technology as much a curse as a blessing? (Asimov, *Robbie* and Bradbury, "The Veldt").

Finally, whenever available, we use film versions of novels, stories, and above all plays, to make them more accessible to today's students who are so visually conditioned. Since a film is itself the interpretation of the screen writer, this book explains how to bring some of these stories to life through comparison-contrast discussion and writing. Together, may we continue to help our students educate their imaginations. Through active and close reading, and viewing film with a critical mind, may we also enable them to become life-long learners.

Sincerely,

Victor and Marc Moeller

1

THE WHAT, WHY, AND HOW OF LITERATURE CIRCLES

"Here in the Midwest, our closely knit team of teachers has been developing one version of literature circles for almost fifteen years.... Do we think our model is better? Certainly not. We are genuinely impressed by the diverse ways that other teachers around the country have created and supported literature discussion groups." (Daniels, 2002)

The first time I saw Harvey Daniels speak was in a large conference room in Wheaton, Illinois. His discussion centered of the nature of reading and how it should develop a sense of the human condition. The teachers I remember most are those who had the ability and courage to tap into the things that really move us: love, relationships, fears, pain, hopes, and dreams. Some teachers, perhaps subconsciously, seem to have been taught to restrict, ignore, or dismiss, the human element in their classrooms. I agree strongly with Daniels's position on the relationship between reading and the human spirit, "We've asked kids to bottle up their responses, and in doing so we have blocked the pathway that leads upward from responding to analyzing and evaluating" (Daniels, 1994, p. 9). With mock humor and irony, Daniels correctly pointed out that presently, "traditional school reading programs are virtually designed to ensure that kids never voluntarily pick up a book once they graduate" (p. 11.)

My father and I regard ourselves among those teachers who have followed the 12 principles of Literature Circles for several years but have made their own refinements and innovations. Literature Circles and Great Book Groups have so much in common that some teachers regard them as a prelude to Great Book Groups while others see them as complementary and still others regard them as an alternative method of engaging all students, *whatever their ability*, in authentic, active learning. However, all teachers agree that both methods, although distinctly different, have common immediate goals: to develop independent and critical thinking and to increase student understanding and enjoyment of literature. Both methods also share the goal of enabling students to become lifelong readers, and as a result, lifelong learners.

TWELVE PRINCIPLES

Two key concepts associated with Literature Circles are independent reading and collaborative learning which were first developed by Becky Abraham Searle. Today, her idea like Harvey Daniels's, is being developed and adapted with great enthusiasm throughout the country. So what are the characteristics of a Literature Circle? Here is our version of the Twelve Principles that determine and guide these small-group discussions.

- ♦ **First**, students choose their own reading.
- ♦ **Second**, small, temporary groups (six to eight students) are formed based on book choice.
- ♦ **Third**, different groups read different books.
- ♦ **Fourth**, groups meet for discussion on a regular, predictable schedule.
- ♦ **Fifth**, group members use written notes to guide both their reading and discussion.
- ♦ **Sixth**, discussion questions come from the students, not teachers or textbooks.
- ♦ **Seventh**, group meetings strive to become open, *natural* conversations about books.
- ♦ **Eighth**, students take on a rotating assortment of role tasks.
- ♦ **Ninth**, the teacher does not lead or participate in group discussions, but acts as a facilitator and observer.
- ♦ **Tenth**, evaluation is by teacher observation and student self-evaluation.
- ♦ **Eleventh**, a spirit of fun about reading pervades the room.
- ♦ **Twelfth**, when books are finished, readers share with their classmates and then new groups form around new reading choices.

Several of these principles need some elaboration. On the **first** principle of letting children choose their own reading, some veteran English teachers may gasp. However, I am not old enough to gasp but agree with Daniels's contention that "you absolutely can not fall in love with a book that someone stuffs down your throat" (Daniels, 1994, p. 19). In my classroom, students are allowed to choose from the books that we have available or are easily obtainable and meet in groups of six to eight with those who have chosen the same book.

The **second** principle, that groups form around book choice, is also vital. I want to group kids the way they would naturally group themselves--out of a common interest. I also realize that I may start off the class with every student picking one book to read for themselves on their own with a regularly scheduled Friday for sustained silent reading, just to get them into the mode of reading for pleasure on their own. Later, I get kids into Literature Circles with a limited list of books from which they can choose and want to read in a group setting. While there is an initial challenge in letting kids choosing their own books and groups, this difficulty can soon be overcome by trial-and-error and common sense.

The **third** principle, allowing kids to choose their books is important for two reasons: it gives them the opportunity to assign reading to themselves as adults do. By giving students the opportunity and practice of setting up their own readings they take ownership. With practice and repetition it may continue even after they leave school. Second, choice is an integral part of literate behavior. Being forced to read too often results in not reading at all—even when one has the freedom to do so. On occasion, the entire class may read and discuss the same book, short story, or play. In this situation, the class is divided into three or four groups of six to eight students.

The **fourth** principle is to have discussions on a regular predictable schedule. As Daniels states, "literature circles require a consistent down payment of time for training, but once they are installed in your portfolio of strategies, they pay big dividends in the reading program all year long" (p. 21). At times, my students meet in Literature Circles weekly, biweekly, or monthly.

The **fifth** principle that kids use written notes to guide both their reading and discussion is essential for the success of the program. By using role sheets (explanation to follow), students have time to respond to the reading before discussion to be able to bring something specific to discussion. Instead of having students fill in correct phrases or answers in workbooks, Literature Circles allow students to reflect and write down their responses *before* discussion. In this way they become genuinely active readers. In addition to preparing students for discussion, notes gathered from these role-playing sheets also serve as a staging area of ideas in the book that can be used by the group for a follow-up project that summarizes main ideas and themes in creative ways: book review, advertising posters, a "missing chapter," or converting parts into readers theater. As a result, students often interest other students in their book.

Principle **six** that discussion questions come from the students, not teachers or textbooks is the life-blood of this method of learning. Indeed, this may be the most important feature of all: "After all, if kids never practice digging the big ideas out of texts themselves and always have teachers doing it for them, how can they ever achieve literary and intellectual independence?" (p. 23). This condition should not be confused with permissiveness or letting kids do whatever they want. When kids are given the opportunity *and* the challenge (thinking *is* difficult) to ask what is really bothering them, they begin to ask *real* questions—those that they have no answer to at all or those that evoke several answers but none of which entirely satisfy. Only real questions lead to an increase in understanding and comprehension. Can we expect students to write good prepared questions spontaneously? Not in our experience. Indeed, some teachers have given up on Literature Circles because their students keep writing factual, trivial, incoherent, or generic questions. (Are they not but imitating the kinds of questions that have been so familiar to them in so much previous reading instruction?)

To ensure productive discussions, teachers must teach mini-lessons on: (1) The difference between factual, interpretive, and evaluation questions. (2) How to formulate good, prepared questions during prediscussion that are *clear, specific, and capable of sustained discussion* because they have multiple implications. (3) How to ask good, spontaneous, follow-up questions for clarification ("Roger, what did you mean by ____?"), substantiation, ("Jennifer, what in the story backs up your idea?"), and more opinion ("Mary, do you agree with John that ____?"). Hence, the coleaders role is to begin discussion with prepared questions and then to develop answers by asking spontaneous follow-ups to move discussion along and to keep it focused on the story.

Principle **seven**, that discussions strive to be open, natural conversations about books, does not mean put-downs, petty comments, bickering or intentional digressions are acceptable. Student coleaders must be taught to deal with rude behavior and to avoid digressions to keep the focus on the book or story. After all, the purpose of discussion, as in Great Book Groups, is to increase understanding and enjoyment of the reading.

Principle **eight**, that students play a rotating assortment of role tasks provides the structure for students to be free to examine their own responses. Since a goal of this kind of discussion is to develop individual responsibility, students must clearly understand the varied roles or tasks that they will assume. These roles should be structured enough so the student is aware of what he or she is to be doing but not so structured as to have a specific outcome in mind. Open-endedness is crucial for lasting results. Daniels stresses that the roles rotate so each student has an opportunity to approach the books from different angles giving them chances to internalize the various perspectives offered by each role. Incidentally, he also advises that once all the students virtually have all of the different roles mastered or memorized that they be phased out and lead into using solely their personal response logs (p. 25.) However, the coleaders' role to prepare and lead good interpretive questions cannot be phased out.

Principle **nine**, that the teacher serves as a "facilitator and observer," sounds like a cliché but not for Daniels. In this setting, the teacher's role is not didactic, to dispense the "correct" interpretation or to correct answers, but to organize, manage, and to handle the logistics. This involves collecting sets of good books, helping groups form, visiting and observing meetings, conferring with kids or groups who struggle, orchestrating sharing sessions, keeping records, making assessment notes, and collecting more books for them to read (p. 26.)

Principle **ten,** evaluation both by teacher observation and student self-evaluation, implies that "covering material," teaching specific "subskills," or "being sure that they get it" (that is, the "correct" interpretation) are all beside the point. According to Daniels, "Literature circles necessitate high order assessment of kids working at the whole thing, the complete, put-together outcome—which, in this case, is joining in a thoughtful small-group conversation about literature" (p. 27). Here authentic assessment by the teacher is through postdiscussion critiques (when the teacher points out what was done well and why and what needs improvement and how to do it), kid watching, narrative observational logs, performance assessment, checklists, student conferences, group interviews, video/audio taping and collecting materials produced in the end of the book group project. Equally important, students are responsible for writing a personal assessment of their own role(s) in the group, record keeping and written summaries and/or resolutions to the discussion questions in brief one-page essays.

Principle **eleven,** that a spirit of playfulness and fun pervade the room, may be a red flag to some principals but not to me. I know the things I learned the most from were almost universally the most fun. In my seventh grade social studies class I was very much involved in the various projects and competitions that made learning fun. In these literature circles I want to create a sense that what they are doing is enjoyable. The fun parts are there. They get to choose the books, thereby choosing the groups. They get to choose roles that are varied and temporary. They get to talk with their friends about what they are reading. They get to design their own "cool" end of the book project that makes the book come alive for them. And then they get to change the book and start all over again.

The **twelfth** principle bears repeating. New groups form around new reading material. There will be a constant mixing in the classroom with different combinations of children being thrown together with each new book choice. This, in effect, may break up groups that have become quite comfortable with each other but I think it is in the best interest of the class to shuffle the groups for developing important social skills and ultimately building a sense of community. Although some hail Literature Circles as a means of detracking, our experience has been that ability grouping is as acceptable as heterogeneous grouping. The issue ought not be that one kind of grouping is better than another but rather accepting that some students function better in one kind of group than another *depending on that group's choice of book.* For example, some students can handle the subtleties of a story like John Updike's "Separating," while others would be mystified. On the other hand, some students may find a story like *Because of Winn-Dixie* not much of a challenge because its meaning is pretty transparent. But what can be done when students choose a book that is too hard or too easy for them? Daniels has two suggestions: the teacher has a private reading conference with the student to select another book or to provide the help (an aide, peer helper, or parent to read parts aloud or even getting the book on tape if possible) necessary for the student to achieve enough understanding to be able to function in his or her group (p. 183).

THE FUNCTION OF ROLE SHEETS IN DISCUSSION

For many teachers who have implemented Literature Circles, five key roles are *required* for success: Discussion Coleaders, Characters Captain, Passage Master, Wordsmith, and a Connector. The Movie Critic's role is optional, of course, depending on the availability of a film version of the story and teacher choice. To illustrate the importance and function of the first five roles, I spend 2 days modeling each task on a short selection (for example, Robert Frost's "The Road Not Taken" or a superb one-page story by William Spencer, "Bethgelert") that the entire class reads to make sure students understand what they will be asked to do in their own groups (pp. 153-157).

The job of the **Discussion Coleaders** is to develop a list of 10 questions for group discussion about the section of the book that has been read prior to their meeting. It is vital that the teacher explains, illustrates, and tests student's understanding about the difference between the three kinds of questions: factual, interpretive, and evaluation. Unless the Discussion Coleaders understanding that they are being asked to write and lead **interpretive** questions, there can be *no increase* in understanding of the reading. Discussion dead-ends when factual questions are raised since they have but one correct answer. Questions of evaluation, those based on personal experience or values, are raised by The Connector, not the Discussion Coleaders.

We have also discovered that coleaders are preferable to a single leader because two students provide more brain power to write good prepared questions, more listening power to ask related spontaneous follow-ups, and more attention power to invite everyone to participate (more or less equally) by calling on them by name and by keeping track on a seating chart. Most importantly, *coleaders ask only questions during discussion*. They do not comment on or judge group responses to avoid turning discussion into an argument or a debate.

The **Characters Captain** lists the major characters in the story, gives a brief description of each one's personality, and explains his or her relationship to the other characters in the story.

The job of the **Passage Master** is to locate two or three key passages of the text that the person thinks the group would like to hear read aloud. The idea here is to help people remember some interesting, powerful, funny, puzzling or important section or sections of the text. The Passage Master's role also involves reading the passage aloud to the group, explaining why it was chosen, and what the group should look for related to it as the reading progresses (p. 78.)

Each group should also have a **Wordsmith** who selects in advance several especially important words that appeared in the reading. These words may be puzzling or unfamiliar, or familiar words that stand out because they are often repeated, used in an unusual way, or are key to the meaning of the text. For example, in Jack Schaefer's classic Western, *Shane*, the word "man" appears 122 times. In nearly every context, it means more than male.

The Connector's role is to find connections between the book the group is reading and the world outside. This means connecting the reading to their own lives, to happenings at school or in the community, to similar events at other times and places, or to other people or problems that the connector is reminded of (p. 80).

Finally, **The Movie Critic's** (sometime) role is to develop a list of at least five important differences between the movie and the original story. The discussion here focuses on whether these changes improve or distort the author's story. In short, would the author agree with these changes? If so, why so? If not, why not?

For teachers who first introduce their students to Literature Circles, a common concern is logistical. For example, a local middle school teacher has written: "If I do writers workshop 4 days a week and literary circles every Friday I'm concerned students may be too rushed, or there may be too much time in between group meetings. As a result, at the outset I will allow more time for training and practice until I'm certain they have the hang of it. Once the roles are familiar and established, I think I can turn them over to developing reading schedules that have them reading 4 days out of 5 and meeting with lots to talk about on that Friday regarding their books. My final logistical concern is the garnering of the books to be used for this project. I have a good number of books at my disposal, however, I am sure I do not have enough. I think possibly I can get parents to subsidize the cost of books if they could contribute a few dollars for them. Also the PTA is very active and generous in the school and perhaps they would be willing to contribute funds for book purchases. I will see how that all goes as the year progresses."

PREPARING STUDENTS TO PARTICIPATE IN LITERATURE CIRCLES: SIX ROLE SHEETS

LESSON PLAN 1

1. Focus:	When was the last time you discussed, really discussed, a book or movie with a friend? Why did you want to talk to someone about that book or movie? (Journal or Response Log)
2. Objective:	To understand the nature and requirements of six roles that participants share in small-group discussions.
3. Purpose:	To prepare students for six different role tasks that they will be asked to perform at different moments during discussion when they gather for a scheduled group meeting.
4. Input and Modeling:	First reading (oral): "The Fox and the Crow" Then (Aesop) and Now (James Thurber, *Fables for Our Time*).
	Second reading (silent): students make notations on whatever is important, whatever they don't understand, whatever they like or dislike, agree or disagree with, and on whatever is related—one part of the story to another (connections).
5. Checking for Understanding:	Review directions on each of the six handouts: Characters Master, Discussion Coleaders, Passage Master, WordSmith, Connector, and Movie Critic (when needed).
6. Guided Practice:	Divide the class into six small groups and assign each group one of the six tasks.
7. Closure:	Review each group's work on each of the six roles. Extol good models and make suggestions for those that need improvement.

HANDOUTS FOR LITERATURE CIRCLES: ROLE SHEETS

1. **Characters Captain:** lists the major characters in the story, gives a brief description of his or her personality, and explains his or her relationship to the other characters in the story.

2. **Discussion Coleaders:** prepares at least five interpretive questions before discussion and asks spontaneous follow-up questions during discussion. The leader also invites each member of the group to contribute what he or she has prepared (passages, vocabulary, and connections).

3. **Passage Master:** selects and reads aloud two or three key passages from the assigned reading, explains why that passage was chosen and then raises questions about them (textual analysis).

4. **Wordsmith:** selects at least five important or unusual vocabulary words and brings them up during discussion when related.

5. **Connector:** prepares at least four questions of evaluation—two based on personal experience and two based on personal values.

6. **The Movie Critic's** role (when a film version is used to follow-up the discussion of a text) is to develop a list of at least five important differences between the movie and the original story.

DISCUSSION COLEADERS
HANDOUT

Name _____ Date _____

Group _____ Class _____

Author _____ Book/Story _____

Discussion Coleader: Your job **before** meeting with your group is to *prepare* a list of **10** good interpretive questions for discussion. (The best questions usually come from your own thoughts, feelings, and concerns as you read the story. Whenever possible, add a page reference that made you think of each question.) Your task **during** discussion is to help your group reflect on, share, and develop its own responses to the reading. You do this during discussion by asking good *spontaneous* follow-up questions for clarification, substantiation, and for more opinion. During discussion you should **also** invite each member to contribute the part that he or she has prepared for discussion: important passages, vocabulary, and connections.

Ten prepared interpretive questions for discussion:

1. _____

2. _____

3. _____

4. _____

5. _____

6. _____

7. _____

8. _____

9. _____

10. _____

PASSAGE MASTER
HANDOUT

Name _____ Date _____
Group _____ Class _____
Author _____ Book/Story _____
Assignment: pp. _____ to _____

Passage Master: Your job is to locate **at least four** special sections of the reading that you think your group ought to read aloud and focus its discussion on. Your job is to help your group focus on two or three interesting, powerful, funny, puzzling, or important passages of the story. You decide which passages or paragraphs are worth hearing and then make a note on how to share them. (You can read passages aloud yourself or ask someone else to read them. After the oral reading, ask each member of the group a question about the passage.

Location   **Reason(s) or choosing this passage**

1. Page ___
      Paragraph _____
2. Page ___
      Paragraph _____
3. Page ___
      Paragraph _____
4. Page ___
      Paragraph _____

Possible reasons for picking a passage to share with your group:

Important	Informative	Surprising	Controversial
Funny	Well-written	Confusing	Memorable
Touching	It is so true	It is so difficult	Thought-provoking

CONNECTOR
HANDOUT

Name _____ Date _____
Group _____ Class _____
Author _____ Book/Story _____
Assignment: pp. _____ to _____

Connector: Your job is to find connections between the book your group is reading and the world outside. List below at least **four questions of evaluation** which connect the reading to your own life, to happenings at school or in the community, to similar events at other times and places, to other people or to problems that you are reminded of. You may also see connections between this book or to others on the same topic or by the same author. Whatever connections you make with the reading based on your own experience or values is what you ought to share with your group.

Questions of evaluation based on personal experience:

1. _____

2. _____

Questions of evaluation based on personal values:

3. _____

4. _____

WORDSMITH
HANDOUT

Name _____ Date _____

Group _____ Class _____

Author _____ Book/Story _____

Assignment: pp. _____ to _____

Vocabulary enricher: Your job is to put your finger on **at least five** especially important words in today's reading. If you find words that are puzzling or unfamiliar, mark them while you are reading and then later jot down their definition, either from a dictionary or some other source. You may also select familiar words that stand out somehow in the reading—words that are repeated often, used in an unusual way, or are key to the meaning of the story. Mark these special words and bring them up during your group discussion whenever they seem related.

Page and paragraph	Word	Definition
1. _____	_____	_____
2. _____	_____	_____
3. _____	_____	_____
4. _____	_____	_____
5. _____	_____	_____
6. _____	_____	_____
7. _____	_____	_____
8. _____	_____	_____

MOVIE CRITIC
HANDOUT

Name _____ Date _____

Group _____ Class _____

Author _____ Book/Story _____

Movie: _____

The Movie Critic's (optional) role is to develop a list of least **five important differences** between the movie and the original story. The discussion will focus on whether these changes improve or distort the author's story. In short, would the author agree with these changes? If so, why? If not, why not? Each difference must be written out as a question that mentions both the movie and the story. For example, "Unlike the novel, why does the movie make the role of Mr. Alfred so much bigger?"

1. _____

2. _____

3. _____

4. _____

5. _____

6. _____

THREE KINDS OF QUESTIONS

LESSON PLAN 2

1. Focus:	What questions do you have about Aesop's fable, "The Fox and the Crow"? (List on the ovehead projector or blackboard at least six questions without comment.)
2. Objective:	To understand by identifying the three types of questions that can be asked about a reading.
3. Purpose:	To prepare the Discussion Leader and the Connector for their roles in discussion.
4. Input and Modeling:	Review handout on the three kinds of questions. Complete with examples on the overhead. Have students copy examples on their copies. First reading (oral) of "The Fox and the Crow" by Aesop and then James Thurber's version.
	Second reading (silent): make notations on whatever is important, whatever you don't understand, whatever you like or dislike, agree or disagree with, or whatever is related—one fable to the other. NOTE: Handouts follow marked (H)
5. Checking for understanding:	Review definitions of the three kinds of questions. Review directions for practice exercise (handout).
6. Guided practice:	Review quiz on the two fables with entire class.
7. Closure:	Return to the list of questions that students raised about the Aesop fable. Point out which questions had but one answer (factual), could be answered more than one way based on the evidence (interpretive), and those that were about personal experience or values (evaluation).
RESOURCES:	Aesop's Fables Online Collection: http://www.pacificnet.net/~johnr/aesop/
	ArtsEdge: Comparing & Contrasting Fables http://artsedge.kennedy-center.org/content/2229/

"THE FOX AND THE CROW"
HANDOUT
Aesop

A Crow stole a piece of cheese, and in order to eat it flew into a high tree. A Fox saw this, so went and sat under the tree, and began to compliment the Crow on her beauty.

"I never noticed before what a delicate white your feathers are!" he exclaimed, "and what a fine and graceful shape your body is. I do not doubt that you have a fairly good voice, but if it is anything like your appearance, I don't know any bird that can compete with you!"

The Crow, flattered by all these compliments, strutted about and preened herself, but feeling that the Fox was a little doubtful of her voice, decided to reassure him as to its beauty, and opened her mouth to sing, dropping the cheese in the process.

This, of course, was what the Fox wanted, so he snapped up the cheese and ran off, laughing at the stupidity of the Crow.

MORAL: *Flatterers cannot be trusted.*

"THE FOX AND THE CROW"
James Thurber

A crow, perched in a tree with a piece of cheese in his beak, attracted the eye and nose of a fox. "If you can sing as prettily as you sit," said the fox, "then you are the prettiest singer within my scent and sight." The fox had read somewhere, and somewhere, and somewhere else, that praising the voice of a crow with cheese in his beak would make him drop the cheese and sing. But this did not happen to this crow in this particular case.

They say you are sly and they say you are crazy," said the crow, having carefully removed the cheese from his beak with the claws on one foot, "but you must be nearsighted as well. Warblers wear gray hats and colored jackets and bright vests, and they are a dollar a hundred. I wear black and I am unique." He began nibbling the cheese, dropping not a single crumb.

"I am sure you are," said the fox, who was neither crazy nor nearsighted, but sly. "I recognize you now that I look more closely, as the most famed and talented of all birds, and while I would be pleased to hear you tell about yourself, I am hungry and must go."

"Tarry awhile," said the crow quickly, "and share my lunch with me." Where-upon he tossed the cunning fox the lion's share of the cheese, and then began to tell about himself. "A ship that sails without a crow's nest sails to doom," he said. "Bars may come and bars may go, but crowbars last forever. I am the pioneer of flight; I am the map maker. Last but never least, my flight is known to scientists and engineers, geometrists and scholars, as the shortest distance between two points. Any two points," he concluded arrogantly.

"Oh, every two points, I am sure," said the fox. "And thank you for the lion's share of what I know you could not spare." And with this he trotted away into the woods, his appetite appeased, leaving the hungry crow perched forlornly in the tree.

MORAL: *'Twas true in Aesop's time, and LaFontaine's, and now—no one else can praise thee quite so well as thou.*

THREE KINDS OF QUESTIONS

"What does it say? What does it mean? Is it true?
Mortimer Adler

When did you first realize the importance of the kinds of questions that you ask your students? Was it when you were puzzled about why some questions fell flat while others provoked immediate response? Was it when you suddenly realized your questions were not clear? Was it when you knew that you placed too much emphasis on factual or memory questions? Was it when you got into "bull sessions" as a consequence of emphasizing evaluative questions? Whatever the moment of insight, few teachers would deny the importance of writing and asking good questions. On the other hand, my experience has been that while teachers recognize that questioning is an art, they also too often are at a loss not only about how to write good discussion questions but also about how to sustain them in discussion.

Mortimer Adler, the eminent American philosopher and education reform leader, first formulated the three kinds of questions in *A Guide for Leaders of Great Books Discussion Groups* (1948). He asked: "(1) What does the author say? (2) What does he mean? (3) Is it true; does it have relevance to you here today? *Fact, Interpretation, Evaluation*--these are the three levels of questions" (p. 8). In 1956, Benjamin Bloom edited a *Taxonomy of Educational Objectives: Cognitive Domain* which classified eight educational objectives that used examples of questions for each kind of thinking: knowledge (memory), comprehension, translation, interpretation, application, analysis, synthesis, and evaluation.

But do teachers need eight kinds of questions? Not in my experience. Too often have I been in workshops where teachers get into vigorous and pointless arguments about identifying types of questions. Bloom's work has its value for developing standardized tests, but for classroom discussion, his added distinctions are not needed since it becomes evident in discussion that translation, application, analysis, and synthesis can be put under the umbrella of interpretation. Knowledge or memory questions are factual and evaluation is about personal values and/or experience. In other words, classroom teachers do well enough, as do most of my colleagues, to recognize the vital difference between *the purpose* of each type of question: to check for recall (factual)?; to check for understanding (interpretation)?; or to check for personal relevance and application (evaluation)?

Here is how I explain and illustrate the three kinds of questions for my students (see handout).

THREE KINDS OF QUESTIONS
HANDOUT

1. **FACTUAL:** A factual question has but one correct answer. It asks the reader to recall something that the author said or to read a passage from the text where an answer can be found. Its answer depends more on memory than thinking.

    For example: Is Thurber's crow black or white?

    Note: Sometimes a factual question does require some thinking to answer correctly but it is still factual because only one answer is possible based on a careful reading of the text.

    For example: Does the crow think he's superior to other birds?

2. **INTERPRETATION:** An interpretive question has more than one correct answer because a difference of opinion about meaning is possible. It asks the reader to explain what the author means by what is said. The answer depends more on thinking than on memory or recall.

    For example: Why does the crow think he is unique when crows are as common as pigeons?

3. **EVALUATION:** An evaluative question asks one to think about his or her own values **or** experiences. Such questions sometimes ask a reader to consider how he or she would act in a situation similar to one a character in the story finds himself of if he or she has had a similar experience.

    For example: (common experience):

    Do you like to talk about your accomplishments?

    For example: (values):

    Do you agree that we are all unique?

NOTE: The **test** for distinguishing between the three types of questions is to begin answering the question itself for a half minute. If you begin talking about the text, the question is factual or interpretive. If it has but one answer, it is factual; if it can be answered in more than one way, *if you have to explain your answer,* it is interpretive. If you begin to talk about your own experiences or values, if you go outside the text, it is evaluation.

THREE KINDS OF QUESTIONS
HANDOUT

"THE FOX AND THE CROW"—EXERCISE 1

DIRECTIONS: First, answer each question briefly in the space beneath it. Second, at the left, identify the type of each question: print FACT for factual, INT for interpretation, and EVAL for evaluation.

_____ 1. Why is the crow white in Aesop but black in Thurber's fable?

_____ 2. Does Thurber's fox know about the Aesop fable?

_____ 3. How does crow insult the fox in Thurber's fable?

_____ 4. Are girls more easily taken in by "sweet talk" than boys?

_____ 5. How does the Fox trick the crow into giving him the cheese in Thurber's fable?

_____ 6. Why does Thurber change the moral of the fable from not trusting flattery to "No one flatters thee quite so well as thou"?

_____ 7. Is self praise more harmful than false praise from others?

_____ 8. Does the crow get the cheese in Aesop in the same way as he does in Thurber's fable?

_____ 9. Is the crow male in Aesop?

_____ 10. Do boys like to brag more than girls?

_____ 11. Why is the crow female in Aesop but male in Thurber?

_____ 12. Why does Thurber repeat the word "somewhere" three times in the third sentence?

QUALITIES OF GOOD QUESTIONS AND BASIC QUESTIONS

LESSON PLAN 3

1. Focus: Why do some questions elicit immediate response and even controversy while others fall flat or meet with apathy or indifference? (Brief discussion or journal topic.)

2. Objective: To illustrate, identify, and write good discussion questions that are clear, specific, interpretive, answerable, and, most importantly, are *real questions*, questions that have the vital element of doubt about the answer.

3. Purpose: ◆ To increase our mutual understanding (comprehension) and, as a result, our enjoyment of the reading.

                     ◆ To develop the habit of independent and critical thinking.

4. Input: Review Six Qualities of Good Discussion Questions (H).

5. Modeling checking, and guided practice: Have students complete (in pairs or individually) Exercise 2 on Qualities of Good Questions. Review as a class what is good about or lacking in each question. A good question will elicit at least two different, plausible answers based on the text.

6. Closure: Review on the OH examples of good student questions that have been revised (previous assignment). Discuss briefly each question to elicit at least two different plausible answers. Ask for supporting textual evidence for each answer.

QUALITIES OF GOOD DISCUSSION QUESTIONS

As a teacher, you must have been puzzled at times about why some questions in class fall flat while others evoke immediate response. While student inattention and unwillingness to think may explain some of the lack of response, we must also look at the quality of the questions that we ask. Some questions are so general or unclear that no one could hope for a reasonable response. In short, those questions that evoke next to no response, may lack one of the important qualities of good prepared discussion questions while those that generate ideas for discussion may have all the necessary qualities. Here is how I explain and illustrate the six characteristics of good discussion questions (handout):

A CHECKLIST ON THE QUALITIES OF GOOD DISCUSSION QUESTIONS
HANDOUT

1. **CLARITY:** A clear question says what it means so that no one has to guess what the questioner has in mind. A question that is not clear is like asking someone to find something but not telling him/her what to look for. *If the question has to be explained or if it cannot be rephrased, it is not clear.* In short, the effort in discussion should be expended on trying to solve the problem, not in trying to figure out the question!

2. **INTERPRETIVE:** Since the primary aim of small-group discussion is to increase the coleader's and the group's understanding of the reading, we focus on questions of interpretation. Factual questions do not generate discussion since they have but one correct answer while questions of evaluation can be answered without even having read the story.

3. **SPECIFIC:** A good discussion question must be specific, that is, tailor-made so that it could be asked only of one reading and not of another. This is not a matter of being picky or merely naming a character but a matter of being precise, that is, of pinpointing *a problem about meaning.*

4. **DOUBT:** There must be doubt in the mind of the person who formulated the question for it to function in discussion. Without the vital element of doubt about the answer to the question, there can be no increase in understanding or insight. A question has the element of doubt **either** when the questioner can think of no answer at all **or**, as is the case more commonly, when the questioner can think of more than one answer but none fully satisfactory. In this case, doubt is a matter of degree; it is not complete. Examples: According to Vonnegust, is the desire to excel as strong as the tendency to mediocrity? (In his "Harrison Bergeron" evidence abounds that supports a yes as well as a no. Hence it is wrong to tell students that "yes and no questions are bad.") Another example: Robert Frost's "The Road Not Taken," raises this issue: Has the choice of the less traveled road been for better or worse? (Again, sufficient evidence in the poem makes yes as plausible as no.)

5. **CARE or CONCERN** about the answer. The coleaders must ask questions that interest them, NOT what they think might interest someone else. This personal quality adds an intensity to a discussion that is lost without it.

QUALITIES OF GOOD DISCUSSION QUESTIONS HANDOUT

"THE FOX AND THE CROW"—EXERCISE 2

Directions: At the left of each question, mark GOOD if it has the qualities of a good discussion question. If the question lacks one of the needed qualities, mark it:

NC if the question is NOT CLEAR
NS if the question is NOT SPECIFIC and could bed asked of any story.
LD for LACKS DOUBT because it cannot be answered in more than one way.
FACT for FACTUAL and cannot be discussed.
EVAL for EVALUATION that could be answered without reading the fables.

_____ 1. What is the main point of each fable?

_____ 2. What do you do when other kids put you down?

_____ 3. What is the relationship between the fox and the crow?

_____ 4. Is the crow in Thurber's fable aware that his praise of himself is funny?

_____ 5. Is Thurber using the fox and the crow?

_____ 6. What are Aesop and Thurber saying about life?

_____ 7. Where does Thurber's fable really take place?

_____ 8. Is Thurber's crow more of a jerk than Aesop's fox?

_____ 9. Does the crow in Thurber's fable regard himself superior to other birds?

_____ 10. What is the meaning of Thurber's moral?

_____ 11. In Thurber's moral, why does he use old word like "thee" and "thou"?

_____ 12. In Thurber's fable, why does the crow *give* his cheese to the fox?

_____ 13. In his fable, why does Aesop want us to know that the crow had stolen the cheese?

_____ 14. In Aesop, why is the crow more concerned about her voice than her good figure?

_____ 15. What does the moral of Aesop's fable mean?

A NOTE ON BASIC INTERPRETIVE QUESTIONS

After students have conducted several discussions, they sometimes notice, sooner or later that some interpretive questions require you to look at many lines and passages of a reading and give rise to a number of other related questions about the author's meaning. Those interpretive questions that consistently lead to sustained discussion (about 20 to 30 minutes per question) are basic questions. Consider the difference between these two questions on "The Fox and the Crow" by James Thurber: (1) Why does the crow think he is unique and (2) Why does Thurber change the moral of the fable from not trusting flatterers to "No one flatters thee quite so well as thou"? Both questions are interpretive but the second is basic. The first question is fairly ease to resolve. You could find a satisfactory answer by pointing out that the crow is able to do many distinctive things or that he's so provincial that he's familiar only with his little world. Someone else could point out that he doesn't know what unique means—that he may think it means only someone special. On the other hand, the second question will evoke many more answers because it has more implications. Another example: In *Because of Winn-Dixie*, Opal, the 10-year-old narrator, hopes for the return of her mother (who had abandoned her at 3) 26 times. So many references lead to this basic question: How does Opal finally learn to accept the truth that her mother will never return? In short, students should be taught the difference between basic and minor interpretive questions to ensure more productive and satisfying discussions.

ON BASIC AND MINOR INTERPRETIVE QUESTIONS HANDOUT

"THE FOX AND THE CROW"—EXERCISE 3

Directions: Which of the questions below are basic and which are minor? At the left, mark **B** if the question is Basic and **M** if you think it is Minor.

_____ 1. Why does Thurber make his crow black and male?

_____ 2. Why does Thurber want us to know that both the fox and the crow are familiar with Aesop's fable?

_____ 3. Unlike the Aesop fable, why does Thurber have the crow *give* his cheese to the fox?

_____ 4. Is Thurber's crow aware that he is being funny and insulting?

_____ 5. Why does the fox in Thurber ignore the insults of the crow?

_____ 6. Why does the fox in Thurber quickly agree with everything that the crow says about himself?

_____ 7. In Aesop why does the fox refer to the crow's stupidity while Thurber describes him as arrogant?

_____ 8. Does Thurber imply that self-praise is more harmful than false praise from others?

_____ 9. Does the crow intend to insult the fox by telling him he's crazy and nearsighted?

_____ 10. After the fox in Thurber gets the cheese, why does he thank the crow as he leaves?

_____ 11. Is the crow joking when he talks about bars and crowbars?

_____ 12. Why does Thurber change the moral of Aesop's fable about not trusting flatterers to "No one can praise thee quite so well as thou"?

ANSWER KEYS

EXERCISE 1:
THREE KINDS OF QUESTIONS

1. INT: You have to figure out the answer for yourself. You cannot look it up in the fable. There are at least two plausible answers to this question based on the story? Can you think of at least one?

2. FACT: Yes, the narrator tells us that the fox had read somewhere that praising the crow's voice would make him drop the cheese.

3. FACT: He says he is crazy as well as nearsighted.

4. EVAL: The answer is a matter of opinion based on *personal experience.*

5. FACT: He pretends that he is hungry and has to leave.

6. INT: This is a basic question of interpretation that has a variety of plausible answers because it has several implications. What would be your answer based on the story?

7. EVAL: The answer is a matter of opinion based on *personal values.*

8. FACT: No. In Aesop the crow drops the cheese when it begins to sing but in Thurber the crow *gives* his cheese to the fox.

9. INT: No. It is female. In the second sentence the fox speaks of "her beauty."

10. EVAL: See answer to question four.

11. INT: See answer to question one.

12. INT: See answer to question one.

EXERCISE 2:
QUALITIES OF GOOD QUESTIONS

1. NS, not specific, because this question can be asked of any story. It is not a *problem* about meaning.

2. EVAL, evaluation, answer is based on personal experience.

3. NS, not specific, can be asked about any two characters in any story. Why do you want to know about their relationship? For example: Do you want to know why the fox ignores the insults of the crow and agrees with everything he says?

4. GOOD, evidence in the fable makes yes as plausible as no.

5. NC, not clear, what does "using" mean? It would have to be explained.

6. NS, no specific. See question 1 comment.

7.   NC, not clear, what does "really" mean? An explanation is needed.

8.   NC, not clear again. The slang word, "jerk" would have to be explained.

9.   LD, lacks doubt. All the evidence points to yes and there is nothing to make no plausible. Better question: Why does the crow think he is unique when crows are as common as pigeons?

10. GOOD in the sense of satisfactory.

11. GOOD because this question is more specific than 10.

12. LD, lacks doubt. The crow wants the fox to stay and listen to him talk about himself. Better question: Why does the fox thank the crow for giving him his cheese?

13. GOOD interpretive question.

14. GOOD interpretive question.

15. LD, lacks doubt. The moral means what it says—"Flatterers cannot be trusted." Better question: Why does Aesop say flatterers "cannot be" rather than "ought not" be trusted?

EXERCISE 3:
ON BASIC AND MINOR INTERPRETIVE QUESTIONS

Questions 4, 8, and 12 are basic because they have multiple implications and would sustain discussion for at least twenty minutes.

Questions 1-3, 5, 6, 7. and 9-11 are minor because they likely have no more than two plausible answers.

Questions 2, 9, and 11 are related (prepared) follow-up questions to basic question 4 about whether the crow knows he is being funny and insulting.

Questions 5, 6 and 10 are related (prepared) follow-up questions to basic question 8 about whether self praise is more harmful than false praise from others.

Questions 1, 3, and 7 are related (prepared) follow-up questions to basic question 12 about why Thurber changes the moral of Aesop's fable.

BETHGELERT
HANDOUT

William Spencer

Prince Llewelyn had a favorite greyhound named Gellert that had been given to him by his father-in-law, King John. He was as gentle as a lamb at home, but a lion in the chase. One day, Llewelyn went to the chase and blew his horn in front of his castle. All his other dogs came to the call, but Gellert never answered it. So he blew a louder blast on his horn and called Gellert by name, but still the greyhound did not come. At last, Prince Llewelyn could wait no longer and went off to the hunt without Gellert. He had little sport that day because Gellert was not there, the swiftest and boldest of his hounds.

He turned back in a rage to his castle, and as he came to the gate, who should he see but Gellert come bounding out to meet him. But when the hound came near him, the Prince was startled to see that his lips and fangs were dripping with blood. Llewelyn started back and the greyhound crouched down at his feet as if surprised or afraid at the way his master greeted him.

Now Prince Llewelyn had a little son a year old with whom Gellert used to play, and a terrible thought crossed the Prince's mind that made him rush towards the child's nursery. And the nearer he came, the more blood and disorder he found about the room. He rushed into it and found the child's cradle overturned and daubed with blood.

Prince Llewelyn grew more and more terrified, and sought for his little son everywhere. He could find him nowhere but only signs of some terrible conflict in which much blood had been shed. At last he felt sure the dog had destroyed his child, and shouting to Gellert, "Monster, thou hast devoured my child," he drew out his sword and plunged it into the greyhound's side, who fell with a deep yelp and still gazing in his master's eyes.

As Gellert raised his dying cry, a little child's cry answered it from beneath the cradle, and there Llewelyn found his child unharmed and just awakened from sleep. But just beside him lay the body of a great gaunt wolf all torn to pieces and covered with blood. Too late, Llewelyn learned what had happened whiled he was away. Gellert had stayed behind to guard the child and had fought and slain the wolf that had tried to destroy Llewelyn's heir.

In vain was all Llewelyn's grief; he could not bring his faithful dog to life again. So he buried him outside the castle walls within sight of the great mountain of Snowdon, where every passer-by might see his grave, and raised over it a great cairn of stones. And to this day, the place is called, Beth Gellert, or the Grave of Gellert, and men say, *I repent me as much as the man that slew his greyhound"* (Spencer, 1998, p. 1811).

2

LITERATURE CIRCLES, THEN (1993) AND NOW (2007): A CRITIQUE

Harvey Daniels deserves enormous credit for developing and spreading literature circles as a most effective method of getting kids hooked on books, turning them into readers who enjoy reading so much that it becomes a daily part of their lives, and, as a result, enabling them to become life-long learners. We are among those teachers like Bonnie Campbell Hill, Nancy Johnson, Katherine Schlick-Noe, Susan McMahon, Katharine Samway, Gail Whang, Jerome Harste, and dozens of others who have not only enthusiastically implemented literature circles in their classrooms but also refined them to the point where they want to pass on to other teachers the benefits of their experience. (For specific titles, see Daniels 2004, chapter 2). In short, we present this book as our "new and improved" version of Literature Circles.

Our goal has been to retain the original strengths of this method of discussion as well as to overcome several of its admitted and common weaknesses and limitations. Most importantly, we have learned that although the teacher does not lead or participate in discussion (Principles 6 and 9) but acts as a facilitator, he or she must, nevertheless, be more active and hands-on to prepare students to participate in and colead discussions. Whenever the teacher is not active *before and after discussion,* too often discussions are neither enjoyable or productive. How, specifically then, can the teacher do more to ensure that everyone has a good experience in literature circles?

Mini-lessons before and after discussion must become a regular part of any effective reading program. A useful book here is *Mini-Lessons for Literature Circles* by Harvey Daniels and Nancy Steineke (2004). Its great strength is its foundation in classroom experience and its practical suggestions for implementation. We too have our own mini-lessons that we explain and illustrate in three lesson plans with handouts in chapter 3. Using the 12 principles of literature circles as an outline, we present here an overview of the ways that we have enhanced our literature circles.

Principle Two: Small groups of four are formed based on book choice.

However, groups of six to eight students often make for better discussion than groups of four. More brain power means more, and often better, ideas for follow-up, consideration, and development. Having discussions lead by coleaders requires small groups of six to eight.

Principle Five: Group members write notes to guide their reading and discussion.

According a colleague, Tom Romano, "Discussion without writing is like cooking without eating." For us, this means learning first how to apply techniques of active and close reading (chapter 2) which not only increase comprehension but also enable students to complete their role sheets.

Principle Six: Discussion questions come from the students, not teachers or textbooks.

To ensure productive discussions, students are taught in mini-lessons:

1. *The difference between factual, interpretive, and evaluation questions.*

2. *During prediscussion, how to formulate good prepared questions that are clear, specific, and capable of sustained discussion because they have the vital element of doubt, that is, questions which have at least two plausible answers or those which have no answer at all (in the minds of the coleaders).*

3. *During discussion, coleaders ask only questions (they do not judge or comment on anyone's response).*

4. *During discussion, coleaders ask spontaneous follow-up questions of substantiation, clarification, and more opinion to move discussion along and to keep it focused on the reading.*

5. *During discussion, coleaders invite everyone to participate (more or less equally) by using a seating chart.*

Principle Seven: Group meetings strive to be open, natural conversations about books.

Nevertheless, the student coleaders avoid digressions and prolonged discussion of evaluation questions to keep the focus on the book since the purpose is to increase understanding and, as a result, enjoyment of the reading.

Principle Nine: The teacher does not lead or participate in group discussions, but acts as a facilitator and observer.

The teacher prepares students in mini-lessons for discussion through a series of exercises on techniques of close and active reading, the three kinds of questions, the qualities of good discussion, writing prepared questions (predis-cussion), asking spontaneous follow-up questions. The teacher also conducts mini-lessons before or after discussion to deal with problems that may arise--lack of preparation, careless completion of role sheets, written self-evaluations (see Daniels & Steineke, 2004).

Principle Ten: Evaluation is by teacher observation and student self-evaluation.

The teacher evaluates literature circles in three ways: grading the role sheets, completing a Criteria for Critique of Discussion sheet, and by grading brief one-paragraph evaluation essays that students write after discussion has been completed on a reading.

ADDENDA

The paragraphs above in italics beneath 6 of the 12 principles of literature circles are specific ways that we have improved and implemented Literature Circles in our classrooms. We also think that these discussion groups can be improved in four other ways:

1. By recognizing that there are wrong answers.* If students are told that there are no "wrong" answers, they will begin to wonder why they should bother about anyone's answer, including their own. Since a purpose of Literature Circles and Great Book groups is to develop independent and critical thinking, students must learn to trust their own judgment about which answers are satisfactory, good, better, best, *and* wrong. How do they do this? By supporting their answers with evidence from the text, by explaining contradictory evidence that other students may raise, and by recognizing that one's personal bias can lead one to misread a story—to read into it something that is not there.

2. By learning how to write and discuss issue questions—that is questions that invite a yes or no answer or that ask for a choice between two opposing alternatives. Examples: According the Vonnegut, is the desire to excel as strong as the tendency to be mediocre? In his "Harrison Bergeron," evidence abounds that supports a yes as well as a no interpretation. Robert Frost's "The Road Not Taken," raises another issue: Has the choice of the less traveled road been for better or worse? Again, sufficient evidence in the poem makes yes as plausible as no response.

3. By recognizing that discussion should begin with interpretation of the book, not personal evaluation. As valid as reader response is in discussion, it should not be the starting point but the concluding point of discussion. Premature evaluation occurs when, for example, students say that something is stupid in a reading before they have made any attempt to understand it. For example, "Harrison Bergeron is a jerk because he invites a ballerina to dance to the ceiling with him." Real and memorable evaluation is often the result of some experience that has been triggered by something that happens in a story. For example, "Now I know what Frost meant when he said he wished he could have taken both roads."

4. By recognizing that ability grouping is as acceptable as heterogeneous grouping in literature circles. The issue ought not be that one grouping is better than another but rather accepting that some students function better in one group than another depending on that group's choice of book. Examples: some students can handle the subtleties of a short story like John Updike's "Separating," while others would be mystified. On the other hand, some students may find a story like *Because of Winn-Dixie* not much of a challenge because its meaning is pretty transparent.

*"While Probst and Rosenblatt both agree that there are better and worse readings of texts, *there are no 'wrong' ones*. Any work of literature is always a confrontation, a collaboration, between a reader's prior experience and words of an author" (Daniels, 1994, pp. 34-35).

In her classic *Literature as Exploration*, Rosenblatt (1968) makes clear that although one's personal experience colors and determines to some extent one's interpretation of a story, she also insists that *there is no one correct interpretation* but several since evidence supports a variety of view points. *However,* she does not deny that *there are wrong interpretations.* Wrong interpretations occur when: (1) the bias of our personal experience leads us to misread a text, that is, to read into it something that is not there; (2) nothing in the text supports our interpretation; and/ or (3) evidence in the text contradicts our interpretation that cannot be explained.

3

TECHNIQUES OF
ACTIVE AND CLOSE READING

"The person who does not spend at least as much time in *actively* and definitely thinking about what he has read as he has spent in reading, is simply insulting the author."

—Arnold Bennett

A first step for participating in a Literature Circle is reading the selection. Far too many students read neither actively nor closely—not only because they have not learned how to discriminate among the various purposes of different kinds of reading but also because they have not been taught how to read actively. Here is a method that I have found productive if employed continually by teacher and student.

The phrase "active and close reading" suggests immediately two ideas. First, some books and stories deserve to be read closely, slowly, and actively—not only because we would miss many of their implied meanings but also because we must learn to recognize meanings other than our own in what we peruse. Second, there are times when how fast we read or how much we read is of no importance. What IS important is that we learn **to reflect** on what we read and learn how to carry on a conversation with the author. We converse with an author when we always question the text.

The purpose of active and close reading is to learn to read interpretively—to pay attention not merely to WHAT an author says but to WHY he says it in the WAY that he does. In short, the purpose in reading is not merely trying to recall what happens in a story, for example, but to think about why things happen as they do. With nonfiction, active readers take particular note of an author's choice of words (diction), use of sentence structure (syntax), and his or her organization of ideas.

Some books and stories like those that we will be reading, can be **interpreted in several ways.** And no individual, adult or child, teacher or student, ever thinks of ALL of the possible interpretations in a given selection. As a result, no one can tell you what is THE correct interpretation of a story, poem, or play—not even, believe it or not, not even the author! However, this does NOT mean that all interpretations are equally good or correct. On the contrary, some interpretations are better than others and some are wrong. How can this be so? The answer is that some interpretations have more evidence to support them which makes them more plausible. Other interpretations are more comprehensive, that is, they explain more of a text than does another view. Still other interpretations are wrong: either there is no evidence to support them or the evidence offered is contradicted by some other statement of the author. But what about the author, why doesn't he or she have the last word about what was "really meant"? Thomas Mann (1969), in the extraordinary afterword of his novel, "The Making of *The Magic Mountain*," says: "I consider it a mistake to think that the author himself is the best judge of his work. He may be that while he is still at work on it and living in it. But once done, it tends to be something he has got rid of, something foreign to him; others, as time goes on, will know more and better about it than he. *They can often remind him of things in it he has forgotten or indeed never quite knew.*"

Just as no one can tell you what is THE correct interpretation nor what your interpretation must be, so also no one can tell you **what details** in your reading are important. Meaning can begin anywhere—even with what someone else might regard an insignificant detail. Whatever furnishes you with clues for arriving at your own interpretation, that is what is important. In short, what is important varies from reader to reader.

In addition, to interpret a work for yourself does NOT require that you first read about the author's life, or about the times in which the author lived, nor review general introductory or background statements. Instead, a reader can begin by noting his responses to a story and then try to convert as many of them as possible into questions. But to engage in this process fruitfully, a reader must learn to respect his own responses—that is, to take seriously his thoughts and feelings about a book.

Forming good questions whose answers can yield a great deal of meaning about a story requires at least **two readings.** Roland Barthes (1975), the eminent French literary critic, maintains that "He who reads a story only once is condemned to read the same story his whole life" (p. 101). On the **first reading**, the reader's main interest should be to note his responses in writing, that is, to make notations. Tom Romano, a New York high school English teacher, says that "Reading without writing [here, notations] is like cooking without eating" (p. 205). During the **second reading**, readers note new responses and pay special attention to those notations that they can convert into questions.

Unless a reader learns to put his or her responses into writing by making notations as she reads, she will have few questions—or, if there are any questions at all, they will be so general that they could be asked of any story. Such generic questions yield little new knowledge and yet without questions, no one can increase his understanding of the material. The first step to learning then is, paradoxically, knowing what you want to know—that is, asking real questions.

As American philosopher and educator Mortimer Adler (1940a) explains in his classic essay on "How to Mark a Book," a notation is any response to the text that a reader puts into writing. **Notations take various forms:**

1. <u>Underlining</u> what is important.

2. Vertical lines at the margin (to emphasize a statement already marked).

3. Star, asterisk, or other doodad in the margin (to be used sparingly to emphasize 10 or 20 most important statements in the book).

4. Numbers in the margin (to indicate the sequence of points the author makes in developing a single argument).

5. Numbers of other pages in the margin (to indicate where else in the book the author makes points relevant to the point marked—to make conenctions among related ideas—drawing lines between sentences).

6. Circling key words or phrases and unfamiliar vocabulary.

7. Comments in the margins: personal, emotional reactions, agreements, and disagreements.

8. Questions in the margins (carrying on a conversation with the author. Note which of your questions the author may answer as well as those that he does not answer.

9. Use self-stick memo pads of various sizes for longer notes and para-phrases.

10. Use the front and end pages to make an index of related ideas and out-line or overview of the authors organization of ideas.

As John Ruskin so aptly remarked, "No book is worth anything which is not worth much; nor is it serviceable until it has been read and reread, and loved, and loved again, *and marked.*" Serviceable is the key word.

Experienced readers have found that whenever they mark up a text, they usually refer to one or more of **four sources** for formulating questions:

1. **Whatever they think is important** (for whatever reason).

2. **Whatever they don't understand.** Not understanding something is more than circling unfamiliar vocabulary (although it includes this). It also means making notations about a character's motivation, for exam-ple, or why the story begins or ends as it does, or what the author means by a certain statement or includes a certain scene, and so on.

3. **Whatever they like or dislike, agree or disagree with.** In other words, active readers are also careful to note their emotional responses. For

Louise Rosenblatt (1968, part II), this step is crucial—what the reader brings to the text.

4. **Whatever they think is related**—one part of the text to another. A chief concern of the second reading is looking for connections or patterns among various parts of the reading. For example:

   ◆ The repetition of the same word or phrase.

   ◆ The reoccurrence of similar actions.

   ◆ Contrasting words or actions.

   ◆ The place of something in the text (organization).

As with so many things, whatever we get out of an enterprise is proportionate to the effort we put into it. So too with reading. Unless we learn how to become thoughtful, active, and close readers, we will continue to miss many of the implications of what we read and, as a result, lose the pleasure of increasing our understanding of the text.

On the next page, consider the notations that were made on a well-known poem by Robert Frost that illustrate the four sources and the various forms of notations. On the second reading, note which of these responses led to discussion questions.

THE ROAD NOT TAKEN
HANDOUT
Robert Frost
[1847-1963]

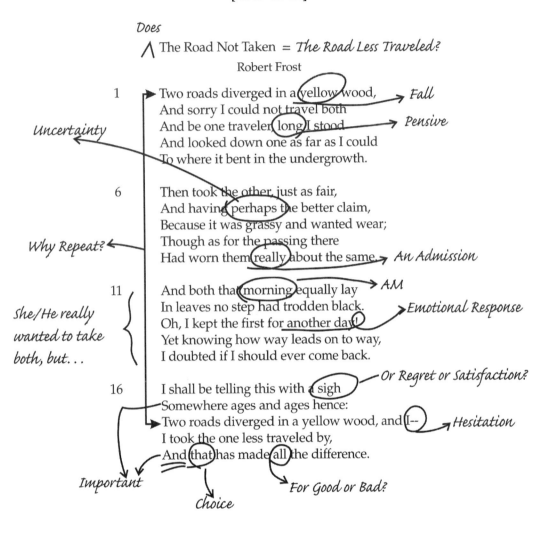

Does

∧ The Road Not Taken = *The Road Less Traveled?*

Robert Frost

Uncertainty

1 Two roads diverged in a yellow wood,   → *Fall*
And sorry I could not travel both
And be one traveler long I stood,   → *Pensive*
And looked down one as far as I could
To where it bent in the undergrowth.

Why Repeat?

6 Then took the other, just as fair,
And having perhaps the better claim,
Because it was grassy and wanted wear;
Though as for the passing there
Had worn them really about the same.   → *An Admission*

She/He really wanted to take both, but...

11 And both that morning equally lay   → *AM*
In leaves no step had trodden black.   → *Emotional Response*
Oh, I kept the first for another day!
Yet knowing how way leads on to way,
I doubted if I should ever come back.

— Or Regret or Satisfaction?

16 I shall be telling this with a sigh
Somewhere ages and ages hence:
Two roads diverged in a yellow wood, and I--   → *Hesitation*
I took the one less traveled by,
And that has made all the difference.

Important   *Choice*   *For Good or Bad?*

FIRST READING: NOTATIONS FOR OVERHEAD

1. Whatever you think important:

    The narrator really would like to have taken both roads (line 3).

    The narrator admits the two roads were really about the same (line 10)

    The narrator is talking about a major decision (line 16)

2. Whatever you don't understand.

    Why isn't the title about the road less traveled?

    Why will the speaker be telling about his decision with a sigh?

3. Whatever you like or dislike, agree or disagree with.

    Whenever I make an important decision, I too sometimes wonder what would have happened if I had chosen differently.

4. Whatever you think is related:

    ♦   The repetition of the same word or phrase.
        First and eighteenth line.

    ♦   The reoccurrence of similar actions.
        Choosing to look back on a previous choice.

    ♦   Contrasting words or actions.
        Speaking about a decision and making that decision.

    ♦   The place of something in the text (organization).
        Which word(s) of the last line need(s) emphasis?

SECOND READING: NOTATIONS CONVERTED INTO QUESTIONS

1. Why isn't the title of the poem "The Road Less Traveled"?

2. Why is the choice of the less traveled road made on a fall morning? (lines 1 &11)

3. Why would the narrator like to have taken both roads? (lines 2 & 13)

4. Why does the narrator say that one road had "perhaps" the better claim? (line 7)

5. Why does the narrator admit the two roads were really much the same? (line 10)

6. Why is there an exclamation point at the end of line 13?

7. Does the narrator sigh out of satisfaction or regret? (line 16)

8. Will the narrator be telling of his choice to others or only to himself? (line 16)

9. Why does the narrator think he will be speaking of his decision in the distant future? (line 17)

10. Why does line 18 end with a dash?

11. Is the narrator beginning to doubt his choice of the less traveled road? (line 18)

12. Has the choice of the less traveled road been for the better or the worse?

ON READING NONFICTION

But what about nonfiction? Do these active reading techniques for fiction apply equally to nonfiction? Yes and no. The same basic techniques of making notations, writing questions, and so on apply also to nonfiction which is commonly defined as "all forms of prose that purport to be factual" and use exposition, argumentation, and fictions only to illustrate. However, with factual prose, particular attention must be given to (1) identifying the author's thesis (what) and purpose (why); (2) his audience (who); (3) his style (how) of writing—diction, syntax, vocabulary, and use of examples; (4) the structure and organization of ideas; (5) the relationships among the principal sections of the text; and (6) above all, his tone or attitude toward his topic must be determined. As the College Board people continually remind us, "to miss the tone is to miss the meaning."

See an overview of the five themes in Chapter 4 and introductions to these related, nonfiction, follow-up readings.

4. Who Are Your Real Friends?
   Kate DiCamillo, *Because of Winn-Dixie*—Lesson Plan 4
   Jay Neugeboren, *Luther*—Lesson Plan 5
   Emerson "On Friendship"
   Daniel Pipes, "Black Muslims Inside the U.S."

5. When Do You Need Family Most?
   John Updike, "Separating"—Lesson 6
   Margaret Burr, "Does Love Change?"
   Lorraine Hansberry, *A Raisin in the Sun*—Lesson 7
   Donnellda Rice, "Racial Covenants: A History Past and Present"
   (Carl Hansberry takes redlining to the Supreme Court.)

6. How Important Is a Brother, a Sister, or a Girlfriend in Your Life?
   Carson McCullers, "Sucker"—Lesson 8
   Lorri-Ann, "The Futility of High School Romance"
   Jean Stafford, "Bad Characters"—Lesson 9
   "Why do people shoplift?"
   William Faulkner, "Two Soldiers"—Lesson 10
   A Forum on "What is patriotism?"
   Leo Tolstoy, "Two Brothers"—Lesson 11
   Jill Carattini, "On Happiness"

7. How Do True Leaders Inspire Followers and False Leaders Deceive Theirs?
   George Orwell, *Animal Farm*—Lesson Plan 12
   "Orwell's Allegory of Communism"
   C. S. Lewis, *The Lion, the Witch, and the Wardrobe*—Lesson 13
   "Parallels to the Passion Story in LWW"

8. Is Technology as Much a Blessing as a Curse?
   Ray Bradbury, "The Veldt"—Lesson Plan 14
   "What our homes will look like in 2107"
   Isaac Asimov, *I Robot:* "Robbie"—Lesson Plan 15
   "Sputnik: Dawn of the Space Age—Three Viewpoints"

TEXTUAL ANALYSIS

Textual analysis is a detailed examination of a particular passage in which you try to determine the author's meaning line by line and sometimes word by word. This technique is a good way to get into a reading when the group has not read well enough to participate in an interpretive discussion. In addition to being a remedial device, when teacher and/or student co-leaders use textual analysis, they model what should be happening during the first and second readings. Finally, textual analysis is also effective even when the group is doing well in discussion; in this situation, textual analysis builds on ideas already expressed to draw out more meaning from specific passages that help to resolve the basic question.

Textual analysis involves four steps in this order:

1. **Select a passage** that you want to examine closely and have a group participant real it aloud. Oral reading is not only an important aid to understanding but also an indicator of a student's level of comprehension of what he or she is reading.

2. **Identify the speaker of the passage,** the narrator. It may be the author speaking directly to you, a fictional narrator, an anonymous narrator, or a character speaking to another character.

3. **Identify the context of the passage.** If you have chosen a passage other than the beginning or the conclusion of the story, try to get a rough idea of where you are in the selection. In short, ask questions about what happened just prior to the passage and what happened just after it.

4. **Review the passage line by line and even key words.** This step is the heart of textual analysis and the most important. Go over the difficult passage, line by line freely asking questions of fact or of interpretation about the meaning of words, phrases, and sentences about which you are uncertain of the answer. Freely turn to other sections of the reading that you think are related to the passage being explored. After you have reviewed the entire passage, return to your basic question by restating or rephrasing it and then continue the discussion.

4

WHO ARE YOUR REAL FRIENDS?

In her novel and movie version of *Because of Winn-Dixie*, Kate DiCamillo's 10-year-old narrator, Opal, early on talks to God about how lonely she was in Naomi, Florida because even the kids she did know, the Dunlap brothers, Amanda Wilkinson, and Sweetie Pie Thomas, none wanted to be her friend. However, because of Winn-Dixie, Opal soon makes several unusual friends. Her quest for friendship, raises a basic question about who our real friends are and how it could be that people as unique as Miss Fanny Block, the librarian, Gloria Dump, the neighborhood "witch," Otis, an ex-con, pinched-nose Amanda Wilkinson, and 5-year old Sweetie Pie Thomas, all became genuine friends of Opal. But why? In spite of their many differences, what do they have in common?

Although the movie is 95% faithful to DiCamillo's story, so much so that there can be no question she would approve it, there are four notable differences that raise these questions: (1) Why does the movie open with Opal pretending to play baseball with herself? (2) Why is the role of Mr. Alfred, manager of Friendly Corners Trailer Park, developed into a major character? (3) Why is a police officer added to harass Otis as well as the children? and, (4) Why is the preacher's grace over the food at Gloria and Opal's party moved to the concluding scene?

Those who would like to follow up DiCamillo's story about unlikely friendships with a nonfiction reading may want to use the renowned essay by Emerson on "Friendship." This famous essay introduces students to an author that they have not read and provides them with a challenge to consider his ideas and their relevance to their ideas of friendship.

Jewish author, Jay Neugeboren's "Luther," raises questions about how some teacher's can and do befriend their students. Luther, a student at Booker T. Washington Junior High School in Manhattan, is "different"—so different that his peers avoid him. Colleagues advise his teacher, Mr. Carter, that Luther is "batty" and he ought to "just leave him be." But Luther will not allow Mr. Carter to "just be." These two loaners soon develop a friendship that grows from mutual trust and respect into a life-long friendship. When Luther becomes a Black Muslim, we begin to wonder if Neugeboren has Mr. Carter tell the story of Luther's growing up as a warning of future racial conflict or as the detailed account of how Mr. Carter's friendship enabled Luther to learn how to believe in himself.

BECAUSE OF WINN-DIXIE

LESSON PLAN 4

1. Focus:

    Has an animal or pet ever changed your life in some important way? If so, how? If not, do you know of any one whose life has been changed because of the loyalty or devotion of an animal? (Journal or Response Log)

2. Objective:

    ♦ To understand the nature and requirements of six role sheets on this novel that participants will share in their small-group discussions.

    ♦ To review the Three Kinds of Questions and Qualities of Good Discussion Questions.

3. Purpose:

    To prepare students for small-group discussion.

4. Input and Modeling:

    Plot-check Quiz on Three Kinds of Questions and Exercise on the Qualities of Good Questions on DiCamillo's novel.

5. Checking for Understanding:

    Review the Plot-check Quiz and the Exercise on Qualities of Good Questions.

6. Guided Practice:

    Review the content of each of the six role sheets: Discussion Coleaders, Characters Captain, Passage Master, Connector, and Movie Critic.

7. Closure:

    Extol good examples and make suggestions for those that need improvement.

Source: DiCamillo, K. (2001). *Because of Winn Dixie.* Cambridge, MA: Candlewick Press.

Film: *Because of Winn-Dixie* (DVD) 110 min. Twentieth Century Fox, 2005.

Internet: http://www.imdb.com/title/tt0317132/

BECAUSE OF WINN-DIXIE
PLOT-CHECK QUIZ
HANDOUT
CHAPTERS 1-9

Directions: On your own paper, answer each question briefly in the space beneath it and then identify the type of each question: print FACT for factual, INT for interpretation, and EVAL for evaluation.

_____ 1.   How does India Opal Buloni happen to find Winn-Dixie?

_____ 2.   How does Opal get her father to allow her to keep Winn-Dixie?

_____ 3.   What is one of the 10 important things that her father tells Opal about her mama?

_____ 4.   Why does Opal speak so often about her mama?

_____ 5.   Why does her father allow Opal to bring her dog into the church?

_____ 6.   After Winn-Dixie interrupts the sermon, for whom does Opal ask her congregation to pray?

_____ 7.   After her father's sermon, what does Opal tell God?

_____ 8.   Who becomes Opal's first true friend?

_____ 9.   How does Opal become friends with the person in question 8?

_____ 10.   Why does Opal go to Gertrude's Pet Store?

_____ 11.   After her first visit to Gertrude's store, why is Opal suddenly happy?

_____ 12.   How does Opal happen to meet Gloria Dump?

_____ 13.   How can Gloria Dump see Opal with her heart?

_____ 14.   Based on what you know about Opal in the first nine chapters, would you want to become her friend? If so, how would you go about it? If not, why not?

_____ 15.   How important is God in your life?

BECAUSE OF WINN-DIXIE
REVIEW QUIZ ON QUALITIES OF GOOD QUESTIONS
HANDOUT
CHAPTERS 1-9

Directions: On your own paper, mark GOOD if a question would lead to a disagreement based on the book. If the question lacks one of the needed qualities, mark it:

NC if the question is NOT CLEAR and would have to be explained.
NS if the question is NOT SPECIFIC and could be asked of any story.
LD for LACKS DOUBT since it cannot be answered in more than one way.
FACT for FACTUAL and cannot be discussed.

_____ 1. What kind of relationship do Opal and her father have?

_____ 2. After her father allows Opal to keep Winn-Dixie, why does he say he guessed he would be trouble? (p. 25).

_____ 3. What is the role of Otis in the story?

_____ 4. What if this was a real story and she was only dreaming?

_____ 5. Did Opal's father really love her mother?

_____ 6. Why does Otis give Opal a job in the pet store?

_____ 7. Do the Dewberry brothers believe that Gloria is a witch?

_____ 8. What is the story saying about kids who think they're always right?

_____ 9. Why does Opal memorize the list of ten things that her father told her about her mother?

_____ 10. What is the meaning of the title of the book?

_____ 11. Although Opal loves her father, why does she repeatedly describe him as a turtle? (pp. 16 and 165).

_____ 12. Does Opal ever find out why Amanda is so stuck up?

_____ 13. Why does he just let her go like that?

_____ 14. Why does Opal suggest she and her dog be Miss Fanny's friend?

_____ 15. What does the bear in the library got to with Opal's dog?

ANSWER KEY

PLOT-CHECK QUIZ

1. FACT: She claims him as her own dog when he runs into a Winn-Dixie food store in Naomi, Florida.

2. INT: She at first asks her father a question about the Less Fortunate. She tells him that Winn-Dixie is a stray among the less fortunate (pp. 16-19).

3. FACT: see the list in Chapter Four.

4. INT: Several possible answers: Her mother had abandoned her and her father when she was 3. She cannot understand why her mother would have left her and she hopes continually that her mother will one day return.

5. FACT: To finish his sermon, he orders Opal to bring her dog into the church to stop his howling.

6. FACT: He asks them to pray for the mouse that Dixie had caught.

7. FACT: She tells God that she is lonely and wanted to find some new friends and also prays that the mouse didn't get hurt.

8. FACT: Miss Fanny Block, the librarian.

9. INT: She discovers that Miss Fanny is also lonely because most of her friends were already dead. Significantly, Opal takes the initiative and suggests that they could all be friends. Miss Fanny is delighted.

10. FACT: Opal wants to buy a leash and collar for her dog.

11. FACT: She suddenly realizes that she has a dog, a job, and her first new friend, Miss Fanny.

12. FACT: When Winn-Dixie wanders into her yard, Opal follows him to bring him back home.

13. INT: Since Gloria is nearly blind, when she asks Opal to tell her everything about herself, she says she will have to see her with her heart. Gloria later tells Opal not to judge people by their past but by what they are doing now. Her heart will tell her if she can trust and befriend Opal.

14. EVAL: the question asks for an opinion based on personal experience.

15. EVAL: the question asks for an opinion based on personal values.

ANSWER KEY

REVIEW QUIZ ON QUALITIES OF GOOD DISCUSSION QUESTIONS

1. NS: Not specific since it could be asked of any two characters in any story. See question 11 for a specific question about their relationship.
2. GOOD: He could be making a joke or he could already realize that this dog would become more of a burden than he would be worth.
3. NS: Not specific since it could be asked of any character in any story. See question 6 for a specific question about Otis?
4. NC: Not clear. It is a real story. Who is she? Can you revise?
5. LD: Yes! There's not a bit of evidence that he did not love Opal's mother. Indeed, in Chapter 24 he tells his daughter, "I tried. I tried ... I hoped and prayed and dreamed about [her coming back] for years."
6. GOOD: He is so shy that doesn't know how to say no. Opal takes the initiative and assumes he will give her a job.
7. LD: No. At the party at Gloria Dump's house they tell Opal that they were only kidding.
8. NC: Not clear. What kids think they are always right in this story? Right about what?
9. FACT: She says she did not want to forget them so that if her mama ever did return she would recognize her. (p. 30)
10. NS: Not specific; it can be asked of the title of any book. What do you want to know about the title?
11. GOOD: The word turtle suggests that her father withdraws into himself. She could also mean that he avoid taking responsibility.
12. LD: Yes. Her father tells her that Carson, her 5-year old brother, had drowned.
13. NC: Not clear. Who is he and she? What does "go like that" mean? Question needs explanation. Can you revise?
14. GOOD: Early in the story we learn that Opal is lonely and looking for new friends. Opal soon realizes that Miss Fanny is also lonely.
15. NC: Not clear. What are you asking about Miss Fanny's story? Can you explain?

SUGGESTIONS FOR SIX ROLE SHEETS: CAVEAT

The suggestions for these six role sheets are only that, suggestions. They are NOT to be given to the students since that would be defeat the a major purpose of Literature Circles. According to Principal 6, "Discussion questions [and other ideas in the role sheets] come from the students, not from teachers or textbooks."

Then why offer these ideas at all? So as only to give teachers models of good questions and suggestions that they may sometimes need to come up with when they have a mental block or when they are at a loss for ideas to help their students. In short, these suggestions serve their purpose best when they become a catalyst for a teacher's own ideas and models for their students during mini-lessons before or after discussion.

COLEADER DISCUSSION QUESTIONS: PREPARED QUESTIONS

1. What is "the important thing": about life that Opal learns "because of Winn-Dixie"? (p. 60)

2. Why does Gloria Dump think "the most important thing" is something different for everyone? (p. 96)

3. By the end of the story, what "complicated and wonderful gifts" has Opal discovered in her friends? (p. 153)

4. How does Opal finally learn to accept the truth that her mama will never return? (p. 178)

5. At the end of the story, why is Opal's heart no longer empty over the loss of her mother? (p. 178)

6. By the end of the story, has Opal's or her father's life changed more?

7. What does Opal mean when she says "Just about everything that happened to me that summer happened to me because of Winn-Dixie? (p. 60)

8. In the last chapter, why does the author have Opal examine her tree in Gloria Dump's yard? (pp. 69 & 178)

9. Why does Opal wonder if she seemed like a ghost to her mama just she sometimes seemed like a ghost to her? (p. 97)

10. When Opal prayerfully speaks to her mother, why does she speak of *her father* finally realizing that her mother will not be retuning? (p. 178)

CHARACTERS CAPTAIN

- Setting: Naomi, Florida, 1995 (Mr. Alfred refers to Ebay.)
- India Opal Buloni: the 10-year old narrator whose mother had abandoned her family 7 years ago.
- Winn-Dixie: a stray, a "Less Fortunate" dog that Opal befriends.
- Pastor Buloni: Opal's father (who has no first name); he is pastor of Open Arms Baptist Church who loves his daughter dearly.
- Mrs. Alfred: manager of Friendly Corners Trailer Park. See the Movie Critic's sheet.
- Miss FAnny Block: the librarian of the Merman W. Block Memorial Library.
- Gloria Dump: a near-blind Black woman who the Dunlap brothers regard as the neighborhood witch.
- Otis: the shy ex-con clerk at Gertrude's Pets Store who sings to the animals and gives Opal a job.
- Dunlap (10) and Steve (9) Dewberry: neighborhood boys that harass Opal.
- Amanda Wilkinson: a peer of Opal whose 5-year old brother, Carson, had drowned.
- Sweetie Pie Thomas: a 5-year old who desperately wants her own dog.

WORDSMITH

Many students will not likely have much difficulty with DiCamillo's vocabulary because so much of her language is colloquial. However, some readers may have to look up:

routine (p. 87), *pathological* (pp. 75 & 162), and *desperately* (p. 145).

Are there any other words that would have to be looked up?

PASSAGE MASTER

By far the most important passage for an oral reading and textual analysis is Chapter Twenty-Four (pp. 161-168) when Opal's father wants to give up the search for Winn-Dixie and Opal is so outraged she shouts at her father: "You always give up! You're always pulling your head inside your stupid turtle shell. I bet you didn't even go out and look for my mama when she left." My students respond to this chapter when they hear it as Reader's Theater—when parts have been assigned and read as a dialogue between Opal and her father. As a follow up, I always have the students discuss or write a paragraph on who gave the most dramatic and convincing performance. In other words, which character's emotional expression was more convincing.

CONNECTOR

The Connector's contribution to discussion is to write and raise at least four evaluation questions—two about personal experience and two about personal values. Suggestions:

1. Based on what you know about Opal in the first nine chapters, would you want to become her friend? If so, how would you go about it? If not, why not? (experience)

2. At what moments do you spontaneously let your mama and dad know that you love them? (experience)

3. How important is God in your life? (values)

4. Is there ever anything important enough that you would lie about to your parents? (values)

MOVIE CRITIC

Although the film is 95% true to the Kate DiCamillo's story, so much so that there can be no question she would approve it, there are four notable differences:

1. The film opens with Opal pretending to play baseball with herself. Does this scene set the tone for the story?

2. Mr. Alfred, manager of Friendly Corners Trailer Park, becomes an important minor character who gives Opal's father a special rate out of deference to the church but will not allow Opal to keep a dog. He demands that the preacher calls the pound to remove Winn-Dixie because he did not get rid of him as promised. In a moment of crisis, the preacher has to side with Opal to keep the dog and to eventually convince Mr. Alfred to agree. His reference to getting quotations on Ebay for selling a dog date the film (circa 1995). Mr. Alfred also appears in the concluding scene of the party at Gloria Dump's home. He com-

pletes the picture of how Winn-Dixie had brought together such a disparate group of people. Question: Why is Mr. Alfred developed into an important minor character?

3. The film adds a police officer who appears in two scenes. At first he goes to Gertrude's Pets to hassle Otis about his criminal record. In the second scene he becomes a stereotype of the bumbling cop who disrupts a ball game that Winn-Dixie cuts short because he catches the ball and runs away with it. Question: Why has a policeman been added to the movie version of DiCamillo's novel?

4. The film moves the preacher's prayer before the food is served at Gloria and Opal's party to the closing scene when everyone sings hymns together. At this point, the theme of friendship becomes explicit: "Dear God, we thank you most of all for friends. We appreciate the complicated and wonderful gifts you give us in each other. And we appreciate the task you put down before us, of loving each other the best we can, even as you love us." Question: Why does the movie end with the preacher's prayer unlike the movie which ends with Miss Fanny offering Opal a Littmus Lozenge?

"LUTHER"

LESSON PLAN 5

1. Focus:

Who was *the most unusual and unforgettable* boy or girl student that you have ever met in school? How would you describe his or her physical appearance? How would you describe his or her personality? (Journal or Response Log)

2. Objective:

♦ To understand the nature and requirements of six role sheets on this novel that participants will share in their small-group discussions.

♦ To review the Three Kinds of Questions and Qualities of Good Discussion Questions.

3. Purpose:

To prepare students for small-group discussion.

4. Input and Modeling:

Plot-Check Quiz on Three Kinds of Questions and Exercise on the Qualities of Good Questions on the short story by Jay Nuegeboren.

5. Checking for Understanding:

Review the Plot-Check Quiz and the Exercise on Qualities of Good Questions.

6. Guided Practice:

Review the content of each of the six role sheets: Discussion Coleaders, Characters Captain, Passage Master, Connector, and Movie Critic.

7. Closure:

Extol good examples and make suggestions for those that need improvement.

Source: Neugeboren, J. (1965). *Best American short stories*. New York: Farrar, Straus & Giroux.

Internet: http://www.commonwealmagazine.org/article.php3?id_article=1634

"LUTHER"

PLOT-CHECK QUIZ
HANDOUT

Directions: On your own paper, answer each question briefly in the space beneath it and then identify the type of each question: print FACT for factual, INT for interpretation, and EVAL for evaluation.

_____ 1.   Have you ever written an essay about stealing or something illegal?

_____ 2.   Why does Luther choose to write an essay about stealing fruit?

_____ 3.   Why does Mr. Carter ask Luther where he got the money for baseball tickets?

_____ 4.   How does Luther react to Mr. Carter's comments about his essay on stealing?

_____ 5.   Why does Luther repeatedly turn down Mr. Carter's offer to have coffee or soda together?

_____ 6.   If you could, is there anything that would cause you to quit school?

_____ 7.   Why does Luther think it is okay to disturb Mr. Carter's class?

_____ 8.   Why do some teachers tell Mr. Carter to leave Luther alone?

_____ 9.   What would you do if a close friend was a shoplifter?

_____ 10.   Who taught Luther to "believe in himself"?

_____ 11.   Why does Luther think Mr. Carter took so much interest in him?

_____ 12.   Why is the story told from Mr. Carter's point of view?

_____ 13.   Why does Mr. Carter admit that he didn't know how to help Luther?

_____ 14.   Why doesn't Mr. Carter ever lecture Luther about stealing?

_____ 15.   So far, has any teacher ever made a big difference in your life?

ANSWER KEY

PLOT-CHECK QUIZ

1. Have you ever written an essay about stealing or something illegal?

    EVALUATION: A question about personal experience.

2. Why does Luther choose to write an essay about stealing fruit?

    INTERPRETATION: More than one correct answer is possible depending on evidence in the story.

3. Why does Mr. Carter ask Luther where he got the money for baseball tickets?

    FACT: He wanted to know if he has stolen them. (p. 42)

4. How does Luther react to Mr. Carter's comments about his essay on stealing?

    FACT: He says twice, "Oh, it's superb." (p. 39)

5. Why does Luther repeatedly turn down Mr. Carter's offer to have coffee or soda together?

    INT: More than one correct answer is possible.

6. If you could, is there anything that would cause you to quit school?

    EVAL: A question about personal values.

7. Why does Luther think it is okay to disturb Mr. Carter's class?

    INT: More than one correct answer is possible.

8. Why do some teachers tell Mr. Carter to leave Luther alone?

    FACT: They think that Luther is "batty." (p. 37)

9. What would you do if a close friend was a shoplifter?

    EVAL: A question about personal values.

10. Who taught Luther to "believe in himself"?

    FACT: The Black Muslims. (p. 45)

11. Why does Luther think Mr. Carter took so much interest in him?

    FACT: Luther thought it was because he was Black. (p. 37)

12. Why is the story told from Mr. Carter's point of view?

    INT: More than one correct answer is possible.

13. Why does Mr. Carter admit that he didn't know how to help Luther?

   INT: More than one correct answer is possible.

14. Why doesn't Mr. Carter ever lecture Luther about stealing?

   FACT: He thinks it would have destroyed their relationship. (p. 41)

15. So far, has any teacher ever made a big difference in your life?

   EVAL: A question about personal experience.

Note: Which of these factual questions can be revised as interpretive questions?

"LUTHER"

REVIEW QUIZ ON QUALITIES OF GOOD DISCUSSION QUESTIONS HANDOUT

Directions: On your own paper, mark GOOD if a question would lead to a disagreement based on the story. If the question lacks one of the needed qualities, mark it:

NC if the question is NOT CLEAR and would have to be explained.
NS if the question is NOT SPECIFIC and could be asked of any story.
LD for LACKS DOUBT since it cannot be answered in more than one way.
FACT for FACTUAL and cannot be discussed.

_____ 1. What kind of relationship is there between Luther and Mr. Carter?

_____ 2. Why does Luther think it is okay to steal "when you don't get what you want"?

_____ 3. What is the role of Mr. Carter in the story?

_____ 4. Why does he just let him go like that?

_____ 5. Why does Mr. Carter admit that he didn't know how to help Luther?

_____ 6. What if this was a real story or Luther was only dreaming?

_____ 7. Why doesn't Mr. Carter follow up on Luther's glib answer about why he steals?

_____ 8. What does Luther expect from writing?

_____ 9. What is the story saying about minority students?

_____ 10. Does Mr. Carter help Luther believe in himself before the Black Muslim's did?

_____ 11. What is the meaning of the title of the story?

_____ 12. Does Mr. Carter really care about helping Luther?

_____ 13. Why does Luther have a thing about marriage?

_____ 14. Why do other teachers tell Mr. Carter to leave Luther alone?

_____ 15. Although Mr. Carter avoids lecturing Luther about stealing, why does he refuse to buy a copy of his Black Muslim newspaper?

ANSWER KEY

REVIEW QUIZ ON QUALITIES OF GOOD DISCUSSION QUESTIONS

NC if the question is NOT CLEAR and would have to be explained.
NS if the question is NOT SPECIFIC and could be asked of any story.
LD for LACKS DOUBT since it cannot be answered in more than one way.
FACT for FACTUAL and cannot be discussed.

1. What kind of relationship is there between Luther and Mr. Carter?

    NS: Can be asked of any two characters in any story.

2. Why does Luther think it is okay to steal "when you don't get what you want"?

    GOOD interpretive question for discussion.

3. What is the role of Mr. Carter in the story?

    NS: Can be asked any character in any story.

4. Why does he just let him go like that?

    NC: Who is "he" and who is "him" and what is "like that"?

5. Why does Mr. Carter admit that he didn't know how to help Luther?

    GOOD interpretive question for discussion

6. What if this was a real story or Luther was only dreaming?

    NC: What is the difference between a "real" story and dreaming?

7. Why doesn't Mr. Carter follow up on Luther's glib answer about why he steals?

    GOOD interpretive question for discussion.

8. What does Luther expect from writing?

    NC: What does "expect" mean? What kind of "writing"?

9. What is the story saying about minority students?

    NS: Not enough of a problem. What do you want to know about what the story could be saying about a Black student like Luther?

10. Does Mr. Carter help Luther believe in himself before the Black Muslim's did?

    GOOD interpretive question for discussion.

11. What is the meaning of the title of the story?

    NS: Could be asked about the title of any story.

12. Does Mr. Carter really care about helping Luther?

    LD: Since no evidence supports no, the answer has to be yes.

13. Why does Luther have a thing about marriage?

    NC: What does "thing" mean?

14. Why do other teachers tell Mr. Carter to leave Luther alone?

    FACT: They think he's "batty."

15. Although Mr. Carter avoids lecturing Luther about stealing, why does he refuse to buy a copy of his Black Muslim newspaper?

    GOOD interpretive question for discussion.

SUGGESTIONS FOR SIX ROLE SHEETS: CAVEAT

The suggestions for these six role sheets are only that, suggestions. They are NOT to be given to the students since that would defeat the major purpose of Literature Circles. According to Principal 6, "Discussion questions [and other ideas in the role sheets] come from the students, not from teachers or text-books."

Then why offer these ideas at all? So as only to give teachers models of good questions and suggestions that they may sometimes need to come up with when they have a mental block or when they are at a loss for ideas to help their students. In short, these suggestions serve their purpose best when they become a catalyst for a teacher's own ideas and models for their students during mini-lessons before or after discussion.

COLEADER DISCUSSION QUESTIONS: PREPARED QUESTIONS

1. Unlike other teachers who avoid him, why does Mr. Carter go out of his way to help Luther?

2. Why does Luther tell Mr. Carter that marriage beats stealing? (p. 39)

3. Why does Mr. Carter tell us that the most satisfying time of his 8 years of teaching occurred when Luther began to apply himself in school? (p. 40)

4. Why does Mr. Carter avoid lecturing Luther about stealing to save his relationship with Luther? (p. 41)

5. Why is Mr. Carter almost indifferent to Luther's idea that the All-Star game be replaced with a game between "the white guys against our guys"? (p. 42)

6. Why is Mr. Carter quick to tell Luther that he would have helped him even if he wasn't Black? (p. 42)

7. Does Luther believe that Mr. Carter would have helped him even if he "wasn't colored"? (p. 42)

8. When Mr. Carter visits Luther at reform school, does he fail to live up to Luther's expectations because he doesn't know what they are? (p. 44)

9. Does Mr. Carter help Luther believe in himself before the Black Muslim's saved him? (p. 45)

10. Does the author imply that Luther would not have learned to believe in himself if he had NOT gone to prison twice? (pp. 44-45)

11. Does the author want us to conclude that Luther became a Black Muslim because Mr. Carter could not or did not know how to help him? (p. 44)

12. Why does Mr. Carter refuse to buy Luther's Black Muslim newspaper? (p. 45)

13. Is Mr. Carter sad or worried about Luther becoming a Black Muslim? (p. 45)

14. Does the ending of the story suggest that the 8-year relationship between Luther and Mr. Carter was over? (p. 45)

15. Why does the author end the story with Luther telling Mr. Carter to save the little card that Luther had signed? (pp. 43, 45)

CHARACTERS CAPTAIN

♦ Setting: Booker T. Washington Junior High School, Manhattan, New York, 1955.

♦ Luther: This Black, junior high school student quickly attracts the attention of a beginning teacher, Mr. Carter, not only because of his physical appearance but also because he is so self-absorbed and seemingly unaware of others. However, they soon develop a relationship that continues over several years of ups and downs.

♦ Mr. Carter: As new junior high school teacher, Mr. Carter soon learns to dismiss the opinion of his colleagues that Luther is "batty" and a mental case who he should leave alone. Unlike those teachers who avoid Luther, Mr. Carter goes out of his way to help him for reasons not always clear to him or to Luther.

WORDSMITH

In addition to Luther's favorite word, superb (pp. 39, 42, 44), many students would not likely be familiar with these words: page 37: *trifle, incessant, anecdote*; page 38: *feverishly, competent, disrupt, corridor*; page 40: *suspiciously, furiously, fiend, relieved, frantically*; page 42: *dubiously, flourishing*; page 44: *subdued*; and page 45: *snubbed* and *advocating*.

PASSAGE MASTER

A year after Luther first meets Mr. Carter and Luther becomes a student in his English class, he returns to Mr. Carter's classroom to get his opinion on his four-sentence composition on "How to Steal Some Fruits." Begin with Luther reading his composition (p. 38) and then continue with Mr. Carter's narrative: "The next day he sat quietly in class" and continue until Mr. Carter answers Luther's question: "Okay, Maybe I was thinking that I would like to help you."

My students respond to this passage when they hear it as Reader's Theater—when parts have been assigned and read as a dialogue between Luther and Mrs. Carter. As a follow up, I always have the students discuss or write a journal on: (1) What does the passage reveal about the beginning of Luther and Mrs. Carter's relationship? and (2) Who gave the most dramatic and convincing performance. In other words, which character's emotional expression was more convincing.

CONNECTOR

The Connector's contribution to discussion is to write and raise at least four evaluation questions—two about personal experience and two about personal values. Suggestions:

1. Have you ever had a teacher like Mr. Carter? (experience)
2. Do some teachers try too hard to be your friend? (experience)
3. Had he been in your class, could or would you have become a friend of Luther? If so, how? If not, why not? (values)
4. What would you have said to Luther when he tells Mr. Carter that he steals because "when you don't get what you want, you got to take it"? (values)

MOVIE CRITIC

As a follow-up to this story, you may want to show your students "Finding Forrester"—a related movie about a remarkable and unexpected teacher-student relationship that grew into a life-long friendship. William Forrester, a 70-year-old recluse and renowned author, first encounters Jamal Wallace, a talented Black teenager who lives in the ghetto, as the result of a dare. As their unlikely meeting grows into friendship, we begin to wonder if the title, "Finding Forrester" refers *more* to William Forrester helping Jamal Wallace to discover his future or to Jamal helping Forrester to recover his past?

NONFICTION FOLLOWUP READINGS

♦ A good follow up to the DiCamillo story about unlikely friendships is the renowned essay by Emerson on "Friendship." This long and difficult essay can easily be edited to one or two pages about the two elements of friendship: Truth: *"A friend is a person with whom I may be sincere. Before him I may think aloud"* and Tenderness: *"The only reward of virtue is virtue; the only way to have a friend is to be one."* (Source: Emerson's "Friendship" is in the public domain and can be downloaded at: http://www.rwe.org/index.php?option=com_content&task=view&id=129&Itemid=42)

♦ C. S. Lewis also has a marvelous exposition on friendship in his *The Four Loves* (Chapter IV, Friendship, pp. 87-127). Although lengthy and also intended for mature readers, key paragraphs could easily be assembled and become the basis of a good discussion.

♦ Daniel Pipes, "Black Muslims Inside the U.S." explains why Mr. Carter can be rightly concerned about Luther joining this organization. For additional resources on Black Muslims and Islamic terrorism, access Daniel Piepes's Web site: www.danielpipes.org and The Center for Security Policy at: www.centerforsecuritypolicy.org

5

WHEN DO YOU NEED FAMILY MOST?

John Updike's, "Separating" relates the story of the breakdown of an American family. The pending divorce of Richard and Joan Maples will soon leave its scars in the lives of their four teenage children (Judith 19, Dickie, 17, John 15, and Margaret, "Bean" 13) just when they need family most. As the family begins to disintegrate, Richard becomes responsible for telling the boys and his wife has to tell the girls that "they no longer love each other." Two evident basic questions then arise: (1) Why has Joan and Richard's marriage failed? and, (2) Why is neither parent able to reach out to their children?

The related, follow-up nonfiction reading by Margaret Burr asks, "Does Love Change?" Richard and Joan would answer, "Yes, of course. That is what we told our children. We are separating because we no longer love each other."

In contrast to the Maples family, Lorraine Hansberry's *A Raisin in the Sun* and movie version chronicles how a family saved itself in a moment of crisis that could have torn them forever apart. The Younger family, headed by matriarch Lena, believes that her family might have a way out their "rat trap" in a Black Chicago ghetto. Why? Her late husband, Big Walter's $10,000 insurance money may enable them to "move on up" to a better life. However, each member of the family has his or her own dream: her temperamental son, Water Lee's demeaning job as a chauffeur makes him think the money may be his first and only chance to start his own business—a liquor store. Walter's pregnant wife, Ruth, longs for stability, while Lena's daughter, Beneatha, believes the money would enable her to become a doctor who would someday improve the lives of the hopeless. But it's Lena who has the money and what she wants is something for all of her family: a house with "a whole lot of sunlight"—in an all-White suburb. This moment of crisis raises several basic questions: Does Hansberry imply that the American Dream has been deferred or that it is an illusion? Does Hansberry intend the resolution of her drama to leave us with optimism and hope for the Younger family or with pessimism and uncertainty about its future?

The 1961 film version (B&W, 130 min. VHS) of the play established Sidney Poitier and Ruby Dee as consummate actors. However, the 1990 movie version (160 min. VHS & DVD) with Danny Glover as Walter and Estelle Rolle as Mama is superior because it restores a key scene with Mrs. Johnson (see pages 84-87 for the text) that was censored in the 1961 film. The question is, of course, what made this scene so controversial that it was omitted in 1961?

In her essay on "Racial Covenants," Donnellda Rice explains the origin and the background of Lorraine Hansberry's play: "In 1973, Carl Hansberry bought a home in the Washington Park area of Chicago, an area with a restrictive covenants prohibiting occupancy by Negroes. Supported by the NAACP and his self-run civil rights foundation, Carl Hansberry challenged the restrictive covenant and efforts to force him and his family from their home." As a result, the Supreme Court ruled against the practice of redlining.

"SEPARATING"

LESSON PLAN 6

1. Focus

When do you need family most? (Journal or Response Log)

2. Objective:

♦ To understand the nature and requirements of six role sheets on this short story that participants will share in their small-group discussions.

♦ To review the Three Kinds of Questions and Qualities of Good Discussion Questions.

3. Purpose:

To prepare students for small-group discussion.

4. Input and Modeling:

Plot-Check Quiz on Three Kinds of Questions and Exercise on the Qualities of Good Questions on Updike's short story.

5. Checking for Understanding:

Review the Plot-Check Quiz and the Exercise on Qualities of Good Questions.

6. Guided Practice:

Review the content of each of the six role sheets: Discussion Coleaders, Characters Captain, Passage Master, Connector, and Movie Critic.

7. Closure:

Extol good examples and make suggestions for those that need improvement.

Source: Updike, J. (1987) Separating. In D. Bergman & D. Epstein (Eds.), *The Heath guide to literature* (pp. 260-268). Lexington, MA: D C Heath and Co.

Film: Monterey Home Video, 1986 (95 min.) http://userpages.prexar.com/joyerkes/Item7.html

Internet: http://www.laurahird.com/newreview/updikevcarver.html

Note: Some teachers follow-up this story with Updike's dated but more popular "A & P" (about three girls who go to a supermarket to make a purchase) because it provides such a contrasting tone.

"SEPARATING"

John Updike

PLOT-CHECK QUIZ
HANDOUT

Directions: On your own paper, answer each question briefly in the space beneath it and then identify the type of each question: print FACT for factual, INT for interpretation, and EVAL for evaluation.

_____ 1. Which of the children think it is silly that Richard and Joan do not get a divorce right away rather than wait?

_____ 2. Why are Richard and Joan separating?

_____ 3. Was it Richard's or Joan's idea that they separate?

_____ 4. How do Richard and Joan plan to tell their children about their divorce?

_____ 5. Why is any divorce so often difficult on the lives of the children?

_____ 6. Who is the only one of the children who asks why his parents are separating?

_____ 7. Is Richard serious when he says he would like to undo the separation?

_____ 8. Who is the "boogeyman" that the narrator refers to?

_____ 9. Should parents considering divorce stay together for the sake of the children?

_____ 10. When did Richard first make up his mind to leave Joan?

_____ 11. Why does the narrator refer to Dickie as "Richard's conscience"?

_____ 12. After Joan and Richard tell the children of their separating, why does the narrator say that Richard did not _feel_ separated?

_____ 13. Of the four children, who is the most angry and emotionally upset?

_____ 14. How does Margaret react to the news of the divorce?

_____ 15. Unlike Joan, why does Richard begin blubbering in front of his children when he wants to tell them about the "experiment" to separate for the summer?

ANSWER KEY

THREE KINDS OF QUESTIONS

1. FACT: Judith, their oldest daughter who has just returned from college.
2. INT: Several answers are possible depending on evidence from the story. For example, Richard tells the children he and Joan no longer make one another happy while Joan may suspect "a third person."
3. FACT: It was Richard's idea. Joan tells him: "I couldn't cry I guess because I cried so much all spring. It really isn't fair. It's your idea, and you make it look as though I was kicking you out."
4. FACT: At first Richard wants to tell the boys while Joan would explain it to the girls. However, Joan insists that the children be told together.
5. EVALUATION: The answer depends on personal experience.
6. FACT: In the poignant last paragraph of the story, Dickie asks, his father "Why?"
7. INT: Yes can be as correct as no depending on the evidence from the story.
8. INT: "Boogeyman" is a metaphor that could stand for several things. (p. 263)
9. EVAL: The answer depends on personal values.
10. FACT: It has been "several years" since Richard decided to leave Joan.
11. INT: Several answers are possible that depend on the story.
12. INT: Several answers are possible that depend on the story.
13. FACT: John angrily wants to know why his parents didn't tell them that they weren't getting along and says they don't care about them— "We're just the little things you had!"
14. FACT: After telling John to stop showing off, Margaret withdraws into herself and resorts to silence.
15. INT: Several answers are possible that depend on the story.

"SEPARATING"

REVIEW QUIZ ON QUALITIES OF GOOD QUESTIONS
HANDOUT

Directions: On your own paper, mark GOOD if a question would lead to a disagreement based on the book. If the question lacks one of the needed qualities, mark it:

NC if the question is NOT CLEAR
NS if the question is NOT SPECIFIC and could be asked of any story.
LD for LACKS DOUBT since it cannot be answered in more than one way.
FACT for FACTUAL and cannot be discussed.
EVAL for EVALUATION that could be answered without reading the story.

_____ 1. What is Updike's purpose in writing this story?

_____ 2. Why are the Maples separating?

_____ 3. Why don't they tell their kids the truth?

_____ 4. Why does Joan insist on telling the children one on one?

_____ 5. Why does Dickie react they way he does?

_____ 6. What does the tennis court mean?

_____ 7. Does Updike show a relation between the fact that Judith was without a tan and unemotional in the beginning of the story and the last paragraph? (pp. 260, 268)

_____ 8. Have you ever been embarrassed by your father's conduct at home or in public?

_____ 9. Why does Updike spend so much time on description instead of getting to the point?

_____ 10. Why does Richard act like a jerk?

_____ 11. Why does Updike end the story with Richard unable to answer his oldest son's question, Why?

_____ 12. What is the message of the story?

_____ 13. Why has Judith not been home for a year?

_____ 14. Does Dickie really care about his parents separation?

_____ 15. How do the children react to the news of their parent's separating?

Answer Key

Qualities of Good Questions

1. NS: The question could be asked of any story.

2. GOOD: It will generate an extended discussion because it involves so much of the story.

3. NC: What is "the truth"? It would have to be explained.

4. FACT: Joan insists that the children be treated as individuals, not as members of a "corporation."

5. NC: What reaction? Explanation needed.

6. NC: Again, what can a tennis court mean other than being a tennis court?

7. NC: What does the question mean? What does Judith's lack of a tan have to do with the beginning and end of the story?

8. EVAL: The answer depends on personal experience, not the story.

9. NS: What description, specifically?

10. NC: What do you mean by a "jerk"?

11. GOOD: It will generate an extended discussion since it involves so much of the story.

12. NS: The question could be asked of any story.

13. FACT: Judith has been away at college.

14. LD: All the evidence points to yes.

15. FACT: Each one of the children reacts in his or her own way. See pages 263-264.

SUGGESTIONS FOR SIX ROLE SHEETS: CAVEAT

The suggestions for these six role sheets are only that, suggestions. They are NOT to be given to the students since that would defeat the a major purpose of Literature Circles. According to Principal 6, "Discussion questions [and other ideas in the role sheets] come from the students, not from teachers or textbooks."

Then why offer these ideas at all? So as only to give teachers models of good questions and suggestions that they may sometimes need to come up with when they have a mental block or when they are at a loss for ideas to help their students. In short, these suggestions serve their purpose best when they become a catalyst for a teacher's own ideas and models for their students during mini-lessons before or after discussion.

COLEADER DISCUSSION QUESTIONS: PREPARED QUESTIONS

1. Why does Updike end the story with Richard forgetting why he and Joan are separating?

2. Are we to believe the narrator that Richard has forgotten the reason for separating? (p. 268)

3. Are Richard and Joan separating because of a third person? (pp. 265, 267)

4. Why is it Richard's idea to leave Joan? (p. 265)

5. Why was Dickie the only one of the children who asked why his parents were separating? (p. 268)

6. Why does the narrator refer to Dickie as Richard's conscience? (p. 265)

7. Why is Richard pleased that the children did not question why their parents are separating? (p. 265)

8. Why does Richard say he would like to be able to undo the separation? (p. 265)

9. Why does Richard think that he is unable to stop the separation? (p. 265)

10. What is "the white face" that the narrator refers to at the end of the story? (pp. 261, 268)

CHARACTERS CAPTAIN

♦ Setting: The Maples' walk from Tenth Street to Washington Square took them through the Greenwich Village area of New York City. It is summer during the late 1980s.

♦ Richard Maples is a middle-aged father who seems never to have matured. His inability to control his emotions and confused motivation for wanting a divorce make him a rather pathetic adult.

♦ Joan Maples appears to be the stable member of the family. She has more or less resigned herself to the divorce and wants to get on with her life and her family.

♦ Judith is the oldest daughter, 19, who has just come home from college. She thinks that her parents are "silly" to delay getting a divorce.

♦ Dickie is the oldest son, 17, who is the only one to ask his father why he is divorcing his mother.

♦ John is the youngest son, 15, who is so emotionally disturbed by the news of his parents divorce that he reveals a spectrum of emotions. He flips out, shouts, ate a cigarette, and made a salad out of the napkin.

♦ Margaret, also known as "Bean," is the youngest who withdraws into herself and becomes silent.

WORDSMITH

Although many students will likely have difficulty with Updike's sophisticated vocabulary, there are only a few words that may interfere with a reader's understanding. For example: *imprudence* (p. 260), *celebratory* (p. 262), *sophisticated* (p.263), *grimace* (p. 263), *conspiratorial* (p. 263), *boogeyman* (p. 263), *tersely* (p. 263), *pachysandra* (p. 264), *mollified* (p. 264), *savoring* (p. 266), *precipitous* (p. 266), and *palpable* (p. 266).

PASSAGE MASTER

Richard's painful attempt to properly tell his oldest son, Dickie, that he and his mother are about to get a divorce is the climax of the story. (pp. 267-268)

CONNECTOR

Some middle school teachers regard the topic of divorce as so painful for those children who have already experienced it that they omit the connector's role in this discussion. However, many high school teachers think that 11th and 12th graders are emotionally stable enough to discuss its effects in their own or their friends' lives.

A Raisin in the Sun

Lesson Plan 7

1. Focus:

When did you need your family most? (Journal or Response Log)

2. Objective:

- ◆ To understand the nature and requirements of six role sheets on this play that participants will share in their small-group discussions.
- ◆ To review the Three Kinds of Questions and Qualities of Good Discussion Questions.

3. Purpose:

To prepare students for small-group discussion.

4. Input and Modeling:

Plot-Check Quiz on Three Kinds of Questions and Exercise on the Qualities of Good Questions on short story.

5. Checking for Understanding:

Review the Plot-Check Quiz and the Exercise on Qualities of Good Questions on the play.

6. Guided Practice:

Review the content of each of the six role sheets: Characters Captain, Discussion Coleaders, Passage Master, Wordsmith, Connector, and Movie Critic.

7. Closure:

Extol good examples and make suggestions for those that need improvement.

Source: Hansberry, L. (1958). *A raisin in the sun.* New York: New American Library.

Film: Sidney Poitier & Ruby Dee, *A Raisin in the Sun* (1961), B&W/130 min. VHR
Danny Glover & Estelle Rolle, *A Raisin in the Sun* (1990), Color/160 min. VHR

Internet: http://www.bookrags.com/notes/rai/

A RAISIN IN THE SUN

PLOT-CHECK QUIZ
HANDOUT

Directions: On your own paper, answer each question briefly and then identify the type of each question: print FACT for factual, INT for interpretation, and EVAL for evaluation.

_____ 1. Does the Younger family disagree about the importance of money in their lives?

_____ 2. If you found a wallet with $1,000 dollars and a driver's license in it, would you return it?

_____ 3. Why does Walter think he is a volcano and a giant surrounded by ants?

_____ 4. Why is Ruth so unhappy living in the ghetto?

_____ 5. Although she doesn't like him, why does Beneatha date George Murchison?

_____ 6. Why doesn't Beneatha believe in God?

_____ 7. Do you believe in God? If so, which God?

_____ 8. Why doesn't Beneatha realize that her view of God is so offensive to Mama?

_____ 9. Why does Walter's dream of owning a liquor store fall apart?

_____ 10. Why does Karl Linder offer to buy Mama's new house?

_____ 11. Would you be insulted if someone called you a dreamer?

_____ 12. Why does Beneatha think her dream of becoming a doctor is gone because Walter wasted her insurance money?

_____ 13. What reason does Walter give Linder for not selling him their new house?

_____ 14. Why is Ruth so determined to get out of the ghetto?

_____ 15. Although the insurance money is gone, why does Hansberry still have the Younger family move into their new home?

ANSWER KEY

PLOT-CHECK QUIZ

Directions: On your own paper, answer each question briefly and then identify the type of each question: print FACT for factual, INT for interpretation, and EVAL for evaluation.

1. Does the Younger family disagree about the importance of money in their lives?

    FACT: Yes, for Walter money is what life is all about. (p. 61) For Mama and Ruth it is their ticket out of the ghetto, and for Beneatha it will enable her to become a doctor. (pp. 16, 29, 31, 40, 43, 55-57, and 76)

2. If you found a wallet with $1,000 dollars and a driver's license in it, would you return it?

    EVAL: This is a question about personal honesty, a moral value.

3. Why does Walter think he is a volcano and a giant surrounded by ants?

    INT: Several explanations are possible based on the evidence.

4. Why is Ruth so unhappy living in the ghetto?

    FACT: She is entirely frustrated because she cannot see any way that her family can find a better life. (p. 73)

5. Although she doesn't like him, why does Beneatha date George Murchison?

    INT: Several explanations are possible based on the evidence. (p. 37)

6. Why doesn't Beneatha believe in God?

    FACT: "God is just one idea I don't accept ... I'm tired of Him getting credit for all the things the human race achieves ... There simply is no God—there is only man and it is he who makes miracles!" (p. 39)

7. Do you believe in God? If so, which God?

    EVAL: This is a question about personal a moral value.

8. Why doesn't Beneatha realize that her view of God is so offensive to Mama?

    INT: several explanations are possible based on the evidence. (p. 40)

9. Why does Walter's dream of owning a liquor store fall apart?

    FACT: Willy Harris stole Walter's part of the insurance money.

10. Why does Karl Linder offer to buy Mama's new house?

> FACT: Linder is a benevolent racist who believes that races should remain segregated because "Negro families are happier when they remain in their own communities." (p. 98)

11. Would you be insulted if someone called you a dreamer?

> EVAL: This is a question about a personal value.

12. Why does Beneatha think her dream of becoming a doctor is gone because Walter wasted her insurance money?

> INT: Several explanations are possible based on the evidence. (p. 113)

13. What reason does Walter give Linder for not selling him their new house?

> FACT: "We have decided to move into our house because my father—my father—he earned it, brick by brick." (p. 128)

14. Why is Ruth so determined to get out of the ghetto?

> INT: Several explanations are possible based on the evidence. (p. 79)

15. Although the insurance money is gone, why does Hansberry still have the Younger family move into their new home?

> INT: several explanations are possible based on the evidence. (pp. 127-130)

A Raisin in the Sun

Review Quiz on Qualities of Good Questions Handout

Directions: On your own paper, mark GOOD if a question would lead to a disagreement based on the book. If the question lacks one of the needed qualities, mark it:

NC if the question is NOT CLEAR
NS if the question is NOT SPECIFIC and could be asked of any story.
LD for LACKS DOUBT since it cannot be answered in more than one way.
FACT for FACTUAL and cannot be discussed.
EVAL for EVALUATION that could be answered without reading the story.

_____ 1. What is the meaning of the title of Hansberry's play?

_____ 2. What does Mama mean when she tells Walter that Ruth is thinking about getting rid of the baby?

_____ 3. Why does Walter finally accept Beneatha's dream of becoming a doctor?

_____ 4. Why doesn't Ruth want to talk to Walter?

_____ 5. At first, why doesn't Walter think it is wrong to deal with Linder?

_____ 6. What is the purpose of the role of George Murchison in the play?

_____ 7. What is the connection between Beneatha's atheism and Walter's liquor store?

_____ 8. Why does Walter treat George Murchison like a moron?

_____ 9. Why does Hansberry have Walter want to own a liquor store rather than some other kind of business?

_____ 10. Is Linder serious about offering to buy Mama's new house?

_____ 11. Why do Walter, Ruth, and Beneatha fight so much?

_____ 12. What does Beneatha mean when she tells Asagai that there should be more than one feeling between a man and a woman?

_____ 13. What goodness does Beneath eventually discover in Asagai that would make her want to marry him?

_____ 14. What does Beneatha think that Mama and Walter came around to?

_____ 15. What is Asagai's purpose in the play?

ANSWER KEY

REVIEW QUIZ ON QUALITIES OF GOOD QUESTIONS

NC if the question is NOT CLEAR
NS if the question is NOT SPECIFIC and could be asked of any story.
LD for LACKS DOUBT since it cannot be answered in more than one way.
FACT for FACTUAL and cannot be discussed.
EVAL for EVALUATION that could be answered without reading the story.

1. What is the meaning of the title of Hansberry's play?

    NS: Can be asked of any title of any story.
    Revision: Why is Hansberry's title a reference to Langston Hughs'
    poem, "A Dream Deferred"?

2. What does Mama mean when she tells Walter that Ruth is thinking
    about getting rid of the baby?

    LD: She means she may have an abortion. (p. 61)

3. Why does Walter finally accept Beneatha's dream of becoming a doc-
    tor?

    GOOD interpretive question for discussion.

4. Why doesn't ruth want to talk to Walter?

    NS: About what? Do you have a page reference?

5. At first, why doesn't Walter think it is wrong to deal with Linder?

    LD: At this point in the play, Walter still thinks that money is every-
    one's first and only concern in life. For once, he says, "The tooken is
    going to be a taker." (p. 61)

6. What is the purpose of the role of George Murchison in the play?

    NS: Can be asked of any character in any story.
    Revision: What makes Beneatha conclude that George is a fool?

7. What is the connection between Beneatha's atheism and Walter's
    liquor store?

    NC: How can there be any connection between the two? If a ques-
    tion has to be explained or if it cannot be rephrased, it is not clear.

8. Why does Walter treat George Murchison like a moron?

    NC: What does "moron" mean in this question? George is an intelli-
    gent, arrogant, and wealthy snobbish young man. *How* does Walter
    treat him like a "moron"?

9. Why does Hansberry have Walter want to own a liquor store rather than some other kind of business?

    GOOD interpretive question for discussion.

10. Is Linder serious about offering to buy Mama's new house?

    LD: Yes! There can be no doubt since all the evidence supports yes.

11. Why do Walter, Ruth, and Beneatha fight so much?

    NS: What do they fight about—specifically? Do you have a page?

12. What does Beneatha mean when she tells Asagai that there should be more than one feeling between a man and a woman?

    GOOD interpretive question for discussion. (p. 50)

13. What goodness does Beneath eventually discover in Asagai that would make her want to marry him?

    GOOD interpretive question for discussion.

14. What does Beneatha think that Mama and Walter came around to?

    NC: "Came around to" what? What does this question mean?

15. What is Asagai's purpose in the play?

    NS: Can be asked of any character in any story.

SUGGESTIONS FOR SIX ROLE SHEETS: CAVEAT

The suggestions for these six role sheets are only that, suggestions. They are NOT to be given to the students since that would defeat a major purpose of Literature Circles. According to Principal 6, "Discussion questions [and other ideas in the role sheets] come from the students, not from teachers or textbooks."

Then why offer these ideas at all? So as only to give teachers models of good questions and suggestions that they may sometimes need to come up with when they have a mental block or when they are at a loss for ideas to help their students. In short, these suggestions serve their purpose best when they become a catalyst for a teacher's own ideas and models for their students during mini-lessons before or after discussion.

CHARACTERS CAPTAIN

- Setting: South side Chicago, sometime between World War II and the present (1959).

- Lena (Mama) Younger (Claudia McNeil/Esther Rolle*): The matriarch and guiding light of the family. Hansberry dedicated her play "To Mama: in gratitude for the dream."

- Big Walter Younger: Mama's deceased husband. She recalls his words: "Seems like God didn't see fit to give the black man nothing but dreams-but He did give us children to make them dreams seem worthwhile? His insurance money enables the Younger family to move into a new home in the suburbs. (p. 33)

- Walter Lee Younger (Sidney Poitier/Danny Glover)": The desperate, entirely frustrated son of Big Walter wants to make something of his life: "I'm thirty-five years old. I been married eleven years and I got a boy who sleeps in the living room-and all I got to give him is stories about how rich white people live. (pp. 22, 121)

- Ruth Younger (Ruby Dee/Starletta DuPois): Like her husband, she too is frustrated living in the ghetto that she is determined to leave-at whatever the cost. (pp. 20, 79)

- Travis Younger (Glynn Turman/Kimble Joyner): The 10-year-old son of Walter and Ruth.

- Beneatha (Diana Sands/Kim Yancey): An idealist who wants to join a Godlike profession, to become a doctor who can save and restore lives of children. When her brother squanders her money for school, she bitterly concludes that "Man is foul." (p. 114)

- Joseph Asagai (Ivan Dixon/Lon Ferguson): Beneatha's boyfriend from Nigeria serves as an evident contrast to George Murchison. Asagai becomes Beneatha's counselor and confidant when she is about to abandon her dream of becoming a doctor. Beneatha's idealism and bitterness is tempered by Asagai's realism and faith in future progress.

- George Murchison (Louis Gossett/Joseph Phillips): George, Beneatha's early boyfriend, attempts to mold Beneath into his chauvinistic image of a servile woman. As he reveals his true values, Beneatha soon realizes that George is a fool.

- Mrs. Johnson (censored/Helen Martin): According to Beneatha, "If there are two things we, as a people, have got to overcome, one is the Klu Klux Klan—and the other is Mrs. Johnson. Her role was so controversial in 1959 that it was omitted in the stage and first film version (1961). However, her visit to the Younger family just as they are about to move into their new home was restored in the 1991 film.

♦ Karl Linder (John Fields/John Fields): This benign racist of the New Neighbors Orientation Committee appears in both the 1961 and 30 years later in the 1991 film version.

♦ Bobo: (Lonne Elder/Stephen Henderson): A drinking buddy of Walter who allows Willy Harris to run off with the insurance money of the Younger family.

Note: *The first character's name in (_____) refers to the 1961 movie, the second the 1991 film.

COLEADERS DISCUSSION QUESTIONS: PREPARED QUESTIONS

1. Does Hansberry intend that the conclusion of her play leaves us with a sense of optimism and hope for the Younger family or with a feeling of pessimism and uncertainty about its future?

2. Does Hansberry want us to agree with Karl Linder's opinion "that you can't change people's hearts" on racial matters? (p. 99)

3. Although Beneatha planned to be a doctor before the insurance money arrived, why does she give up on her dream after the money is gone? (p. 113)

4. Why doesn't Mama stop Walter when he tells her that he plans to sell out to Karl Linder? (p. 126)

5. Even after the loss of the money, why does the Younger family still plan to move into their new home? (p. 127)

6. When Walter tells "the man" that he will not sell out to him, why does Hansberry have Linder reply, "I sure hope you know what you are getting into"? (p. 128)

7. Throughout the play, why does Hansberry keep drawing our attention to Mama's plant? (pp. 27, 40, 101, 130)

8. Does Beneatha plan to marry Asagai and move to Africa to help his improve the lives of his people? (p. 129)

9. Why does the play end with Mama's comment that Walter Lee finally came into his manhood? (p. 130)

10. Why does Mama compare Walter's newfound manhood to a rainbow? (p. 130)

11. Why is the last scene of the play Mama returning to their old apartment to get her plant? (p. 130)

12. Why does Hansberry have the happiness of the Younger family depend on Mama's wisdom?

PASSAGE MASTER

1. Restored scene: Mrs. Johnson's visit just after Mama has purchased a house in all-White Clybourne Park. Conduct as a Readers' Theater (see end of lesson).

2. Asagai and Beneatha's argument about their future: Act III, pp. 110-118.

3. Resolution: Mama and Beneatha's conversation: Mama, "Ain't it the truth … to the last sentence. (pp. 128-130)

WORDSMITH

Although most students will not likely have particular difficulty with Hansberry's vocabulary, the following list of words should be looked up:

assimilationist (pp. 49, 63, 67)   *sophisticate* (p. 47)

heritage (p. 68)   *viciously* (p. 17)

entrepreneur (p. 117)   *conspicuously* (p. 17)

deferred (poem)   *radiantly* (p. 77)

episode (p. 50)   *idealist* (p. 112)

neurotic (p. 37)   *realist* (p. 114)

snobbish (p. 37)   *forlornly* (p. 45)

Prometheus (p. 72)   *Titan* (p. 117)

CONNECTOR

1. Do you know of any family that has had such a big disagreement that it almost fell apart?

2. When do you need family most?

3. Do you agree with Robert Frost's definition of a home as "the place where, when you have to go there, they have to take you in"? If so, why? If not, why not?

4. When is your family happiest? When is it the saddest?

MOVIE CRITIC

1. Why was the scene with Mrs. Johnson omitted in the 1961 film but restored in the 1991 movie? (Act II, Scene 2, p. 84)

2. Why was the scene with Travis and his friends killing a rat ("as big as a cat") also omitted in the 1961 film but restored in the 1991 movie. (Act I, Scene 2, p. 46)

A RAISIN IN THE SUN
HANDOUT
ACT II, SCENE 2

NOTE: This scene, Mrs. Johnson's visit to the Younger family just after Mama's purchase of a house in all-White Clybourne Park, was cut from the original 1959 production and censored in following editions of the play. The 1990 film version of the play restores the entire scene. The basic question is, of course, why was this scene omitted in the 1961 film but restored in the 1991 film?

BENEATHA: Mama—
MAMA: Yes, baby—
BENEATHA: Thank you.
MAMA: For what?
BENEATHA: For understanding me this time [that George Murchison is a fool]. (p. 84)
(She exists quickly and the mother stands, smiling a little looking at the place where Beneatha just stood. Ruth enters)
RUTH: Now don't you fool with any of this stuff, Lena—
MAMA: Oh, I just thought I'd sort a few things out. Is Brother here?
RUTH: Yes.
MAMA: *(With concern)* Is he—
RUTH: *(Reading her eyes)* Yes.
(Mama is silent and someone knocks at the door. Mama and Ruth exchange weary and knowing glances and Ruth opens it to admit a neighbor, Mrs. Johnson, who is a rather squeaky wide-eyed lady of no particular age, with a newspaper under her arm)
MAMA: *(Changing her expression to acute delight and a ringing cheerful greeting)*
Oh-hello there, Johnson.
JOHNSON: *(This is a woman who decided long ago to be* enthusiastic *about* everything *in life and she is inclined to wave her wrist vigorously at the height of her exclamatory comments)*
Hello there, yourself! H'you this evening, Ruth?
RUTH: *(Not much of a deceptive type)* Fine, Mis' Johnson, h'you?
JOHNSON: Fine. *(Reaching out quickly, playfully, and patting Ruth's stomach)* Ain't you starting to poke out none yet! *(She mugs with delight at the overfamiliar remark and her eyes dart around looking at the crates and packing preparation; Mama's face is a cold sheet of endurance)*
Oh, ain't we getting ready round here, though! Yessir! Lookathere! I'm telling you the Youngers is really getting ready to move on up a little higher! Bless God!

MAMA: *(A little drily, doubting the total sincerity of the Blesser)*
Bless God.

JOHNSON: He's good, ain't He?

MAMA: Oh yes, He's good.

JOHNSON: I mean sometimes He works in mysterious ways … but He works, don't He!

MAMA: *(The same)* Yes, he does.

JOHNSON: I'm just soooooo happy for y'all. And this here child—*(About Ruth)* looks like she could just pop open with happiness, don't she. Where's all the rest of the family?

MAMA: Bennie's gone to bed—

JOHNSON: (Ain't no … (The implication is pregnancy) sickness done hit you—I hope …?

MAMA: No-she just tired. She was out this evening.

JOHNSON: *(All is a coo, an emphatic coo)* Aw-ain't that lovely. She still going out with the little Murchison boy?

MAMA: *(Drily)* Ummmmm huh.

JOHNSON: That's lovely. You sure got lovely children, Younger. Me and Isaiah talks all the time 'bout what fine children you was blessed with. We sure do.

MAMA: Ruth, give Mis' Johnson a piece of sweet potato pie and some milk.

JOHNSON: Oh honey, I can't hardly stay a minute—I just dropped in to see if there was anything I could do. *(Accepting the food easily)* I guess y'all seen the news what's all over the colored paper this week …

MAMA: No—didn't get mine yet this week.

JOHNSON: *(Lifting her head and blinking with the spirit of catastrophe)* You mean you ain't read 'bout them colored people that was bombed out their place out there? *(Ruth straightens with concern and takes the paper and reads it. Johnson notices her and feeds commentary)*

JOHNSON: Ain't it something how bad these here White folks is getting here in Chicago! Lord, getting so you think you right down in Mississippi *(With tremendous and rather insincere sense of melodrama)* 'Course I thinks it's wonderful how our folks keeps on pushing out. You hear some of these Negroes around here talking 'bout how they don't go where they ain't wanted and all that—but not me, honey! *(This is a lie)* Wilhemenia Othella Johnson goes anywhere, any time she feels like it! *(With head movement for emphasis)* Yes I do! Why if we left it up to these here crackers, the poor niggers wouldn't have nothing— *(She clasps her hand over her mouth)* Oh, I always forgets you don't 'low that word in your house.

MAMA: *(Quietly, looking at her)* No—I don't 'low it.

JOHNSON: *(Vigorously again)* Me neither! I was just telling Isaiah yesterday when he come using it in front of me—I said, "Isaiah, it's just like Mis' Younger says all the time—"

MAMA: Don't you want some more pie?

JOHNSON: No-no thank you; this was lovely. I got to get on over home and have my midnight coffee. I hear some people say it don't let them sleep bit I finds I can't close my eyes right lessen I done had that laaaast cup of coffee ... *(She waits. A beat. Undaunted)* My Goodnight coffee, I calls it!

MAMA: *(With much eye-rolling and communication between herself and Ruth)* Ruth, why don't you give Mis' Johnson some coffee. *(Ruth gives Mama an unpleasant look for her kindness)*

JOHNSON: *(Accepting the coffee)* Where's Brother tonight?

MAMA: He's lying down.

JOHNSON: MMmmmmmm, he sure gets his beauty rest, don't he? Good-looking man. Sure is a good-looking man! (Reaching out to pat Ruth's stomach again) I guess that's how we keep on having babies around here. *(She winks at Mama)* One thing 'bout Brother, he always know how to have a good time. And soooooo ambitious! I bet it was his idea y'all moving out to Clybourne Park. Lord—I bet this time next month y'all's names will have been in the papers plenty— *(Holding up her hands to mark off each word of the headline she can see in front of her)* "NEGROES INVADE CLYBOURNE PARK-BOMBED!"

MAMA: *(She and Ruth look at the woman in amazement)* We ain't exactly moving out there to get bombed.

JOHNSON: Oh, honey—you know I'm praying to God every day that don't nothing like that happen! But you have to think of life like it is—and there here Chicago peckerwoods is some baaaad pecker woods.

MAMA: *(Wearily)* We done thought about all that Mis' Johnson
(Beneatha comes out of the bedroom in her robe and passes through to the bathroom. Mrs. Johnson turns)

JOHNSON: Hello there, Bennie!

BENEATHA: *(Crisply)* Hello, Mrs. Johnson.

JOHNSON: How is school?

BENEATHA: *(Crisply)* Fine, thank you. *(She goes out)*

JOHNSON: *(Insulted)* Getting so she don't have much to say to nobody.

MAMA: The child was on her way to the bathroom.

JOHNSON: I know—but sometimes she act like ain't got time to pass the time of day with nobody ain't been to college. Oh—I ain't criticizing her none. It's just—you know how some of our young people gets when they get a little education. *(Mama and Ruth say nothing, just look at her)* Yes—well. Well, I guess I better get on home. *(Unmoving)* 'Course I can understand how she must be proud and everything—being the only one in the family to make something of herself. I know just being a chauffeur ain't never satisfied Brother none. He shouldn't feel like that though. Ain't nothing wrong with being a chauffeur.

MAMA: There's plenty wrong with it

JOHNSON: What?

MAMA: Plenty. My husband always said being any kind of a servant wasn't a fit thing for a man to have to be. He always said a man's hands was made to make things, or to turn the earth with—not to drive nobody's car for 'em—or— *(She looks at her own hands)* carry they slop jars. And my boy is just like him—he wasn't meant to wait on nobody.

JOHNSON: *(Rising, somewhat offended)* Mmmmmm The Youngers is too much for me! *(She looks around)* You sure one proud-acting bunch of colored folks. Well—I always thinks like Booker T. Washington said that time—"Education has spoiled many a good plow hand"—

MAMA: Is that what old Booker T. said?

JOHNSON: He sure did.

MAMA: Well it sure sounds just like him. The fool.

JOHNSON: *(Indignantly)* Well—he was one of our great men.

MAMA: Who said so?

JOHNSON: *(Nonplussed)* You know, me and you ain't never agreed about some things, Lena Younger. I guess I better be going—

RUTH: *(Quickly)* Good night.

JOHNSON: Good night. Oh— *(Thrusting it at her)* You can keep the paper! *(With a trill)* 'Night.

MAMA: Good night, Mis' Johnson. *(Mrs. Johnson exits)*

RUTH: If ignorance was gold …

MAMA: Shush. Don't talk about folks behind their backs.

RUTH: You do.

MAMA: I'm old and corrupted. *(Beneatha enters)* You was rude to Mis' Johnson, and I don't like it at all.

BENEATHA: *(At her door)* Mama, if there is are two things we, as a people, have got to overcome, one is the Klu Klux Klan—and the other is Mrs. Johnson. *(She exits)*

MAMA: Smart aleck. *(The phone rings)*

RUTH: I'll get it.

MAMA: Lord, ain't this a popular place tonight. (p. 84)

RUTH: (At the phone) Hello—Just a minute. *(Goes to the door)* Walter, it's Mrs. Arnold.

NONFICTION FOLLOWUP READINGS

♦ Among many related readings on divorce, "Doll" asks Margaret "Peg" Burr, "Does Love Change?" Burr is a licensed marriage family therapist with a private practice in Santa Clarita, CA. Her advice column can be downloaded at: http://www.queendom.com/advices/advice.htm?advice =177

♦ Donnellda Rice, in her essay on "Racial Covenants," explains the origin and background of Lorraine Hansberry's experience with redlining in Chicago: "In 1973, Carl Hansberry bought a home in the Washington Park area of Chicago, an area with a restrictive convenants prohibiting occupancy by Negroes. Supported by the NAACP and his self-run civil rights foundation, Carl Hansberry challenged the restrictive covenant and efforts to force him and his family from their home." As a result, the Supreme Court ruled against the practice of redlining. A further conse- quence, is Lorraine Hansberry's play, the first Black dramatist to win the Best Play of the Year Award in 1958. Donnellda Rice, Esq. practices in Virginia. Her essay can be accessed at http://www.drylongso.com/ specialdelivery/artricles/racial-covenants.html

6

HOW IMPORTANT IS A BROTHER, A SISTER, OR A GIRLFRIEND IN YOUR LIFE?

In Carson McCuller's story, "Sucker" became the title character because he became Pete's 12-year-old stepbrother as a baby when his parents were killed in an auto accident. Because he was so young, Sucker soon became part of the family of Pete and his kid sisters. Sucker got his nickname because he always remembered and believed whatever Pete said. However, Pete and Sucker's close relationship changed when Pete (16) was a sophomore in high school and became obsessed with winning the attention of an 18-year-old senior, Maybelle Watts. Strangely, there seemed to be a direct connection between these two relationships: when Pete and Maybelle got along so did Peter and Sucker but when problems arose, both relationships soured. And that's what bothers Pete. As he tells his story in retrospect, he is still trying to figure out why he lost Maybelle and, more importantly, his brother Sucker. Hence the story raises this basic question of interpretation: Does Pete look back on his relationship with Sucker to find a solution to their breakup or to excuse his cruel behavior toward Sucker?

Had Pete read Lorri-Ann's essay for her senior English class, "The Futility of High School Romance," he may not have ruined his relationship with Sucker. At least he might have realized that Maybelle did him a favor by dumping him.

Emily Vanderpool and Lottie Jump are the "Bad Characters" in Jean Stafford's poignant story. Of herself Emily says: "I had a bad character, I know that, but my badness never gave me half the enjoyment Jack and Stella [her older brother and sister] thought it did." In contrast, Lottie Jump, Emily's new found friend got plenty of enjoyment from her "badness." Their most unlikely relationship raises four basic questions: (1) Why is Emily fascinated with as well as revolted by Lottie Jump? (2) What is the difference between Emily's "badness" and Lottie's? (3) Does Stafford intend her story to be *entirely* comical and satirical? and (4) Does Stafford give Emily such a sophisticated (grown-up) vocabulary because she is telling the story in retrospect?

Does Lottie Jump shoplift only because she is poor? While that may be one reason, a study by the Sacramento County Sheriff's department, "Why do people shoplift?" concludes that motivations vary as much as individuals and circumstances.

During World War II, when William Faulkner was at the apex of his career as a national author, he wrote two stories, "Barn Burning" and "Two Soldiers." Both stories are told from the viewpoint of 10-year-old narrators—Sarty Snopes and Evan Grier. In "Two Soldiers," much to the dismay of his anxious parents, Evan's 19-year-old brother, Pete, is determined to join the U.S. Army. And Evan is just as determined to join him—regardless of his age. Indeed, Evan runs away from home and begins walking the 80 miles to the army recruiting station in to Memphis. When these two brothers find each other, only then do they realize the depth of their brotherhood. Basic question: Why does Faulkner regard Evan as much a soldier as his brother Pete?

One possible answer to the question is that Faulkner regards Pete and Evan as true patriots. "What is patriotism?" a Forum of *The Nation* magazine (July 15, 1991) offers several answers that are certain to provoke strong responses—negative as well as positive.

A few years before his death, Leo Tolstoy wrote a sequel to his fairy tale, "Ivan the Fool and His Two Brothers"—the fable of "The Two Brothers." The two anonymous brothers could not be more different—the elder is security conscious while the younger is an adventurer and risk taker. When they discover a stone in the forest that assures them happiness if they follow its directions, the brothers disagree about whether or not the stone is a hoax. Although the younger brother invites older brother to join him in the adventure, he declines for several reasons. Five years pass. When the younger brother returns to his older brother's home, they rejoice; however, they again disagree about who has made the better choice. Hence, the basic question: Does Tolstoy want us to believe that the younger or the older brother made the better choice?

In her essay "On Happiness," Jill Carattini compares and contrasts the views of materialist Sigmund Freud and Christian apologist C.S. Lewis. Would either of the two brothers agree with Freud or Lewis's concept of happiness? If so, why? If not, why not?

"SUCKER"

LESSON PLAN 8

1. Focus:

How important is a girlfriend in your life? Have you ever had a girlfriend disrupt your relationships with your mom or dad or with a brother or sister? (Journal or Response Log)

2. Objective:

♦ To understand the nature and requirements of six role sheets on this novel that participants will share in their small-group discussions.

♦ To review the Three Kinds of Questions and Qualities of Good Discussion Questions.

3. Purpose:

To prepare students for small-group discussion.

4. Input and Modeling:

Plot-Check Quiz on Three Kinds of Questions and Exercise on the Qualities of Good Questions on the short story by Carson McCullers.

5. Checking for Understanding:

Review the Plot-Check Quiz and the Exercise on Qualities of Good Questions.

6. Guided Practice:

Review the content of each of the six role sheets: Discussion Coleaders, Characters Captain, Passage Master, and Connector.

7. Closure:

Extol good examples and make suggestions for those that need improvement.

Source: McCullers, C. (1993). Sucker. In *Collected stories of Carson McCullers* (pp. 1-10) Boston: Houghton Mifflin.

Internet: http://www.fantasticfiction.co.uk/m/carson-mccullers/collected-stories-of-carson-mccullers.htm

"SUCKER"

PLOT-CHECK QUIZ
HANDOUT

Directions: On your own paper, answer each question briefly in the space beneath it and then identify the type of each question: print FACT for factual, INT for interpretation, and EVAL for evaluation.

_____ 1. What are Pete's and Sucker's ages and how are they related?

_____ 2. What is the "trouble" that Pete talks about in the opening of the story?

_____ 3. How is Maybelle Watts somehow mixed up in the trouble between Pete and Sucker?

_____ 4. What does Pete tell Sucker about his relationship with Maybelle?

_____ 5. How does Maybelle dump Pete?

_____ 6. How does Pete react to Maybelle's rejection?

_____ 7. How does Pete dump Sucker?

_____ 8. Why was Sucker so hurt by the way that Pete told him off?

_____ 9. How does Sucker react to Pete's rejection?

_____ 10. What explanation does Pete give for not apologizing to Sucker?

ANSWER KEY

PLOT-CHECK QUIZ

1. What are Pete and Sucker's ages and how are they related?

    FACT: Pete is 16 and Sucker 12. Sucker is Pete's cousin but became his adopted brother after Sucker's parents were killed in an auto accident.

2. What is the "trouble" that Pete talks about in the opening of the story?

    INT: An outsider would likely think it is that Pete and Sucker are no longer close to each other. However from Pete's point of view, he may not really understand what exactly this trouble is; his feelings are ambivalent.

3. How is Maybelle Watts somehow mixed up in the trouble between Pete and Sucker?

    FACT: Pete thinks that there may be some connection between Maybelle treating him badly and his meanness towards Sucker.

4. Why does Pete tell Sucker about his relationship with Maybelle?

    INT: Since Pete admits he lies about their relationship ("I made out like it was her who had been running after me all this time"), he may be trying to impress Sucker; on the other hand, he may want Sucker to know that someone else has become important in his life so that Sucker will let him alone and stop being so demanding.

5. How does Maybelle dump Pete?

    FACT: "She told me she was sick and tired of my being around and that she had never cared a rap about me. She said all that."

6. 6. How does Pete react to Maybelle's rejection?

    FACT: "I just stood there and didn't say anything. I walked home very slowly."

7. How does Pete dump Sucker

    FACT: "Why aren't we buddies? Because you're the dumbest slob I ever saw! Nobody cares anything about you! And just because I felt sorry for you sometimes and tried to act decent don't think I give a damn about a dumb-bunny like you! ... Why don't you get a girl friend instead of me? What kind of a sissy do you want to grow up to be anyway?"

8. Why was Sucker so hurt by the way that Pete told him off?

   INT: Pete says it was because his voice was "slow and like I was calm." However, Pete admits that it he does not really understand why Sucker looked up to him so much.

9. How does Sucker react to Pete's rejection?

   FACT: "Sucker didn't move.... Slowly that blank look went away and he closed his mouth. His eyes got narrow and his fists shut. There had never been such a look on him before."

10. Does McCullers want us to believe Pete's explanation for not apologizing to Sucker?

    INT: Yes and no. Pete may be honest when he says "Maybelle was somehow mixed up in what happened." On the other hand, when he confides in the reader, it sounds like he's giving himself an excuse: "You can't help what happens to you at night. That is what made things how they are now."

Note: There are no questions of evaluation.

"Sucker"

Review Quiz on Qualities of Good Questions Handout

Directions: On your own paper, mark GOOD if a question would lead to a disagreement based on the story. If the question lacks one of the needed qualities, mark it:

NC if the question is NOT CLEAR and would have to be explained.
NS if the question is NOT SPECIFIC and could be asked of any story.
LD for LACKS DOUBT since it cannot be answered in more than one way.
FACT for FACTUAL and cannot be discussed.
EVAL for EVALUATION and not about understanding the story.

_____ 1. What kind of relationship is there between Pete and Sucker?

_____ 2. What's the connection between Pete, Sucker, and Maybelle?

_____ 3. Why does Sucker think that Pete doesn't like him anymore?

_____ 4. What's wrong with Sucker?

_____ 5. Why does Sucker do everything Pete tells him even though he isn't stupid?

_____ 6. Do you ever dream about things that you are worried about?

_____ 7. Was Pete out of it?

_____ 8. Why is Pete so upset about telling off Sucker?

_____ 9. What is the meaning of the title?

_____ 10. Does Pete feel bad about hurting Sucker's feelings?

_____ 11. Why does Pete change his mind about introducing Maybelle to Sucker?

_____ 12. Is Pete's problem as big as Sucker's problem?

_____ 13. Should Pete have gotten help when he realizes that he doesn't know how to fix up his relationship with Sucker?

_____ 14. Does Pete feel like a jerk or a fool for having tried to get Maybelle's attention?

_____ 15. In this story is Pete looking for a way to be friends again with Sucker or is he trying to excuse his meanness?

ANSWER KEY

REVIEW QUIZ ON QUALITIES OF GOOD QUESTIONS

Directions: On your own paper, mark GOOD if a question would lead to a disagreement based on the story. If the question lacks one of the needed qualities, mark it:

NC if the question is NOT CLEAR and would have to be explained.
NS if the question is NOT SPECIFIC and could be asked of any story.
LD for LACKS DOUBT since it cannot be answered in more than one way.
FACT for FACTUAL and cannot be discussed.
EVAL for EVALUATION and not about understanding the story.

1. What kind of relationship is there between Pete and Sucker?

    NS: Can be asked of any characters in any story. Furthermore, it can be answered factually: Sucker is Pete's first cousin. In short, the question does not pinpoint a problem about their relationship.

2. What's the connection between Pete, Sucker, and Maybelle?

    NS: Like the first question, this question can be asked of any characters in any story. By the way, merely naming characters does not make the question specific.

3. Why does Sucker think that Pete doesn't like him anymore?

    FACT: He angrily told him to get lost. (pp. 9-10)

4. What's wrong with Sucker?

    NC: What is meant by "wrong"? Do you have a sentence in mind?

5. Why does Sucker do everything Pete tells him even though he isn't stupid?

    GOOD: Several possible explanations are possible depending on the evidence cited.

6. Do you ever dream about things that you are worried about?

    EVAL: A question about personal experience.

7. Was Pete out of it?

    NC: What does "out of it" mean? Slang is always ambiguous.

8. Why is Pete so upset about telling off Sucker?

    GOOD: Several possible explanations are possible depending on the evidence cited.

9. What is the meaning of the title?

   NS: Can be asked of any title. However, in this story Pete explains that the title is a nickname that he gave his cousin, Richard, because "he believed every word I said."

10. Does Pete feel bad about hurting Sucker's feelings?

    LD: Of course. He feels so bad that he becomes obsessed with trying to make up for the hurt that he caused Sucker.

11. Why does Pete change his mind about introducing Maybelle to Sucker?

    FACT: Pete is embarrassed by Sucker's "silly" behavior when he walks into the movie that has already begun.

12. Is Pete's problem as big as Sucker's problem?

    NC: What is each boy's "problem"?

13. Should Pete have gotten help when he realizes that he doesn't know how to fix up his relationship with Sucker?

    EVAL: A question about personal values.

14. Does Pete feel like a jerk or a fool for having tried to get Maybelle's attention?

    LD: Yes, indeed. There is no evidence that he doesn't.

15. In this story is Pete looking for a way to be friends again with Sucker or is he trying to excuse his meanness?

    GOOD: Several possible explanations are possible depending on the evidence cited. This question is basic to the entire story.

SUGGESTIONS FOR SIX ROLE SHEETS:
CAVEAT

The suggestions for these six role sheets are only that, suggestions. They are NOT to be given to the students since that would defeat the major purpose of Literature Circles. According to Principal 6, "Discussion questions [and other ideas in the role sheets] come from the students, not from teachers or textbooks."

Then why offer these ideas at all? So as only to give teachers models of good questions and suggestions that they may sometimes need to come up with when they have a mental block or when they are at a loss for ideas to help their students. In short, these suggestions serve their purpose best when they become a catalyst for a teacher's own ideas and models for their students during mini-lessons before or after discussion.

COLEADER DISCUSSION QUESTIONS:
PREPARED QUESTIONS

Does Pete look back on his relationship with Sucker to find a way to become friends again or to excuse his own actions toward Sucker?

If he wants to be friends again, then:

1. Why does Pete qualify so many statements with "I guess" or "I suppose" or "maybe I would have acted differently"?
2. Does Pete use his experience with Maybelle to excuse his meanness toward Sucker?
3. Is Pete excusing himself when he says what happened at night made things how they are between himself and Sucker?
4. Why does Pete say he couldn't help himself when he told off Sucker?
5. Are we to believe it IS Sucker's fault that Pete cannot apologize to Sucker?

If he is trying to rationalize his conduct, then:

6. Why does Pete admit that he feels guilty that people tend to despise those who admire them a lot?
7. Is Pete sincere when he says he did like Sucker "more than anybody else"?
8. Why does Pete recognize he hurt Sucker so much more because his voice was slow and calm when he told off Sucker?
9. Why does it still bother Pete so much that he can do nothing to get his relationship with Sucker restored?

10.   Why is Pete still uneasy in his mind 3 months after his breakup with Sucker?

CHARACTERS CAPTAIN

♦ Setting: The reference to "a yellow roadster" of a boyfriend of Maybelle places the story in the 1930s when movie theaters were also becoming more prevalent.

♦ Pete: The narrator of the story, is a 16-year-old high school junior whose relationship with a girlfriend, Maybelle, causes him to reject his "adopted" brother, Sucker, and then feels terribly guilty for being so cruel. As a result, he becomes preoccupied with trying to figure out some way to get back in Sucker's favor.

♦ Sucker: He is Pete's 12-year-old first cousin (whose real name is Richard). He was taken in by Pete's parents when Sucker's parents were killed in an auto accident when he was a baby. Richard got the nickname of Sucker because Pete says he "used to always remember and believe every word I said" but adds that "it was not that he was dumb in other ways."

♦ Maybelle Watts: She is a senior in Pete's high school who is almost 18. When Pete begins to vie for the attention of this popular girl, he allows her to take advantage of him. Pete says she acted "like she was the Queen of Sheba and even humiliated me."

WORDSMITH

Since the story is told by a 16-year-old narrator, Pete, McCullers carefully used the vocabulary of an average high school student in the 1930s—so much so, that I could not find a single word that my students of the last 20 years would not likely understand.

PASSAGE MASTER

Two passages, both dialogues, reveal the nature of Pete and Sucker's relationship: (1) When Pete dreams about kissing Maybelle: Begin with: "It was that night when this trouble really started … [conclude with] … make up for the way I had always treated him." (pp. 4-5). And, (2) When Pete tells Sucker off—when, he says "I don't think anybody ever gets that mad but once." Begin with: "Then the finish came between Maybelle and me ... [and end with] "I couldn't help myself or think." (pp. 9-10).

My students respond to these passages when they hear them as Reader's Theater—when parts have been assigned and read as a radio script. As a follow up, I always have the students discuss or write a journal on who gave the most dramatic and convincing performance. In other words, which character's emotional expression was more convincing.

CONNECTOR

The Connector's contribution to discussion is to write and raise at least four evaluation questions—two about personal experience and two about personal values. Suggestions:

1. 1. Have you ever felt stupid for chasing after a girl or a boy? (experience)
2. Are girls more than boys desperate to have friends? If so, why so? If not, why not? (experience)
3. Should parents be more vigilant and careful about their children's friendships? (values)
4. What is your definition of a true friend? (values)

"Bad Characters"

Lesson Plan 9

1. Focus: Have your parents ever warned you to stay away from any "bad characters" in your life? If so, why? What did you do? (Journal or Response Log)

2. Objective:
   - ♦ To understand the nature and requirements of six role sheets on this novel that participants will share in their small-group discussions.
   - ♦ To review the Three Kinds of Questions and Qualities of Good Discussion Questions.

3. Purpose: To prepare students for small-group discussion.

4. Input and Modeling: Plot-Check Quiz on Three Kinds of Questions and Exercise on the Qualities of Good Questions on the short story by Jean Stafford.

5. Checking for Understanding: Review the Plot-Check Quiz and the Exercise on Qualities of Good Questions.

6. Guided Practice: Review the content of each of the six role sheets: Discussion Coleaders, Characters Captain, Passage Master, and Connector.

7. Closure: Extol good examples and make suggestions for those that need improvement.

Sources: Stafford, J. (1964) *Bad characters.* New York: Farrar, Straus. Collected Stories (1969) and "Bad Characters" (pp. 260-285) *Short Stories: Characters in Conflict.* John Warriner, Ed. New York: Harcourt Brace Jovanovich, 1981.

Internet: http://www.fantasticfiction.co.uk/s/jean-stafford/collected-stories.htm
Jean Stafford: http://www.jscheuer.com/stafford.htm

"BAD CHARACTERS"

PLOT-CHECK QUIZ
HANDOUT

Directions: On your own paper, answer each question briefly in the space beneath it and then identify the type of each question: print FACT for factual, INT for interpretation, and EVAL for evaluation.

_____ 1. How do Emily Vanderpool and Lottie Jump first meet?

_____ 2. Why is Emily immediately attracted to and fascinated with Lottie?

_____ 3. What is an important difference between where the Vanderpool and Jump families live?

_____ 4. How does Emily respond when she first finds out that Lottie thinks stealing is a picnic?

_____ 5. After Emily realizes that Emily is "big trouble," why doesn't she avoid her?

_____ 6. Why does Emily betray Lottie in Woolworth's?

_____ 7. Why does Lottie betray Emily at the same time?

_____ 8. Like Emily, would you have betrayed Lottie?

_____ 9. After she has been arrested, why does Emily's father take her to see Judge Bay?

_____ 10. What does Emily learn from this experience with Lottie Jump?

Answer Key

Plot-Check Quiz

Directions: On your own paper, answer each question briefly in the space beneath it and then identify the type of each question: print FACT for factual, INT for interpretation, and EVAL for evaluation.

1. How do Emily Vanderpool and Lottie Jump first meet?

    FACT: Lottie boldly walked into Emily's home to steal a cake. (p. 262)

2. Why is Emily immediately attracted to and fascinated with Lottie?

    INT: A good interpretive question that will evoke several good answers. (pp. 262-64)

3. What is an important difference between where the Vanderpool and Jump families live?

    FACT: Emily lives in the wealthy part of Adams, Colorado while Lottie lives in Arapahoe Creek, the poor section of town. p. 264

4. How does Emily respond when she first finds out that Lottie thinks stealing is a picnic?

    FACT: "Stealing is a sin. You get put in jail for it." (p. 265)

5. After Emily realizes that Emily is "big trouble," why doesn't she avoid her?

    INT: A good interpretive question that will evoke several good answers. (pp. 273, 277)

6. Why does Emily betray Lottie in Woolworth's?

    INT: A good interpretive question that will evoke several good answers. (pp. 278-280)

7. Why does Lottie betray Emily at the same time?

    INT: A good interpretive question that will evoke several good answers. (pp. 280-81)

8. Like Emily, would you have betrayed Lottie?

    EVAL: A question of personal values.

9. After she has been arrested, why does Emily's father take her to see Judge Bay?

    INT: A good interpretive question. (p. 282)

10. What does Emily learn from this experience with Lottie Jump?

    FACT: She began to have more than one friend at a time and "never again when that terrible need to be alone arose did I let fly."

"BAD CHARACTERS":
REVIEW QUIZ ON QUALITIES OF GOOD QUESTIONS
HANDOUT

Directions: On your own paper, mark GOOD if a question would lead to a disagreement based on the story. If the question lacks one of the needed qualities, mark it:

NC if the question is NOT CLEAR and would have to be explained.
NS if the question is NOT SPECIFIC and could be asked of any story.
LD for LACKS DOUBT since it cannot be answered in more than one way.
FACT for FACTUAL and cannot be discussed.
EVAL for EVALUATION and not about understanding the story.

_____ 1. What is Stafford's purpose in writing this story?

_____ 2. Will Emily ever see Lottie again?

_____ 3. Does Stafford intend her story to be entirely comical and satirical?

_____ 4. Do you think the girl figured what was going to happen, happened?

_____ 5. Does Emily think that Lottie is really kinda dumb?

_____ 6. Have you ever embarrassed your parents by doing something illegal?

_____ 7. Does it seem that the judge is trying to guilt the girl for not going to the police?

_____ 8. Why does Stafford give Emily such a sophisticated (grown-up) vocabulary?

_____ 9. What kind of relationship do Emily and Lottie have?

_____ 10. Does the was the deaf and dumb act have something to do with the baby?

_____ 11. Why does Stafford have Lottie rewarded for stealing but Emily shamed and punished?

_____ 12. Does Emily forgive Lottie for getting her in trouble?

ANSWER KEY

REVIEW QUIZ ON QUALITIES OF GOOD QUESTIONS

1. What is Stafford's purpose in writing this story?

    NS: Could be asked of any story.

2. Will Emily ever see Lottie again?

    FACT: She says after her arrest, she never saw her again. p. 281

3. Does Stafford intend her story to be entirely comical and satirical?

    GOOD interpretive question for discussion. Yes can be as correct as no.

4. Do you think the girl figured what was going to happen, happened?

    NC: Which girl? What is "what was going to happen that happened"?

5. Does Emily think that Lottie is really kinda dumb?

    LD: Yes. She sees her brains falling out of her head when she is caught stealing. (p. 280)

6. Have you ever embarrassed your parents by doing something illegal?

    EVAL: A question about personal experience.

7. Does it seem that the judge is trying to guilt the girl for not going to the police?

    NC: Again, which girl? And what does "guilt the girl" mean?

8. Why does Stafford give Emily such a sophisticated (grown-up) vocabulary?

    GOOD interpretive question for discussion.

9. What kind of relationship do Emily and Lottie have?

    NS: Can be asked of any two characters in any story. Note: Merely naming characters does not make a question specific.

10. Does the way the deaf and dumb act have something to do with the baby?

    NC: What "deaf and dumb act" and what would it have to do with a baby? Whose baby?

11. Why does Stafford have Lottie rewarded for stealing but Emily shamed and punished?

     GOOD interpretive question for discussion. (pp. 280-282)

12. Does Emily forgive Lottie for getting her in trouble?

     FACT: No. She says "I hate her to this day." (p. 281)

SUGGESTIONS FOR SIX ROLE SHEETS:
CAVEAT

The suggestions for these six role sheets are only that, suggestions. They are NOT to be given to the students since that would defeat the major purpose of Literature Circles. According to Principal 6, "Discussion questions [and other ideas in the role sheets] come from the students, not from teachers or text-books."

Then why offer these ideas at all? So as only to give teachers models of good questions and suggestions that they may sometimes need to come up with when they have a mental block or when they are at a loss for ideas to help their students. In short, these suggestions serve their purpose best when they become a catalyst for a teacher's own ideas and models for their students during mini-lessons before or after discussion.

COLEADER DISCUSSION QUESTIONS:
PREPARED QUESTIONS

What is the difference between Emily's "badness" and Lottie's?

1. Why does Emily allow Lottie to steal from her own family? (pp. 264, 268-269)
2. Why does Emily think stealing is sinful and unlawful while Lottie regards it as fun and entertainment? (pp. 267, 275)
3. Does Stafford want us to regard Lottie Jump as no more than a petty thief?
4. What does Emily mean when she says that she knows she has a "bad character"? (p. 273)
5. Why does Emily confide in us that her badness never gave her as much enjoyment as Jack and Stella thought it did? (p. 273)
6. Why is Emily not proud to be see with Lottie but proud to be with her? (p. 277)
7. Why does Lottie begin to thing that the whole "enterprise" of stealing is pointless? (p. 279)
8. Why is Emily relieved that she has no part in the actual stealing but still follow Lottie's directions? (p. 275)
9. Why does Emily mention that Lottie was caught twice stealing? (pp. 276, 280)

10. Why does Emily break her friendship with Lottie by telling her she doesn't have any brains? (p. 280)

11. Did Emily plan to have Lottie caught at the dime store?

12. What does Emily mean when she says "if I rooted out all the badness in my, there wouldn't be anything left of me"? (p. 282)

Why is Emily Vanderpool fascinated with and revolted by Lottie Jump?

1. When she first meets Lottie, why is Emily instantly interested in her? (pp. 262-264)

2. Why does Emily promptly befriend Lottie? (p. 266)

3. Why does Emily describe Lottie and "evilly ugly"? (p. 266)

4. Why does Emily feel "brave and lily-livered" when she goes to town with Lottie to steal? (p. 273)

5. After Emily realizes that Lottie is "big Trouble," why doesn't she avoid her? (p. 273)

6. Why is Emily friendship with Lottie the longest she ever had? (p. 273)

7. For what reason does Emily think Lottie betrays her? (p. 280)

8. Why is Emily not proud to be *seen* with Lottie but proud to *be* with her? (p. 277)

9. What kind of "Somebody" is Emily with Lottie? (p. 277)

10. Why does Emily hate Lottie even today? (p. 281)

CHARACTERS CAPTAIN

♦ Setting: Adams, Colorado, 1940s.

♦ Mr. Vanderpool: Emily's father loves Emily dearly and enjoys her sense of humor.

♦ Mrs. Vanderpool: Emily's mother is preoccupied with the new baby, Tess. After Emily is caught shoplifting with Lottie, Emily says she "cried for days because she had nurtured an outlaw."

♦ Emily Vanderpool: In a pensive moment, Emily says of herself: "I had a bad character, I know that, but my badness never gave me half the enjoyment Jack and Stella thought it did." Emily had a habit of throwing a tantrum when even she needed "to be *alone*," or when she knew it gave her an advantage.

♦ Jack Vanderpool: Emily's older brother unknowingly almost "saw glory" when Emily had a butcher knife in her hand and he kept taunting her with "Polecat."

◆ Stella Vanderpool: Emily's younger sister, is "a prig," who insists on calling Emily "Kitty" because of her devotion to Muff, her cat.

◆ Tess Vanderpool: Emily's baby sister.

◆ Lottie Jump: Unlike the upper class wealth of Emily, Lottie Jump (age 11, like Emily) is poor. She lives in Arapahoe Creek, "in a wretched settlement made up of people so poor and so sick that each time Emily passes there she "felt blushed with guilt." Lottie has spent her life living by her wits. Full of spunk and complete self-confidence, her personality immediately mesmerizes Emily. And yet, Emily is revolted by Lottie's stealing.

◆ Judge Bay: A stereotype of the pompous and preachy grown up who scolds Emily for stealing.

◆ Mr. Bellamy: The floorwalker at Woolworth's who catches Lottie shoplifting and is duped by her "deaf and dumb" act. He even believes that Emily is the real thief.

WORDSMITH

Does Stafford give Emily a sophisticated (grown-up) vocabulary because she is telling her story in retrospect (as an adult)? Rephrased: Does 11-year-old Emily use correctly grown-up words because she is telling Emily's story as an adult?

Among other things, does Stafford intend Emily's story to be a vocabulary lesson?

scabbards, vilely, pious, prim, grandiloquent, irrevocable, invective, alienated (p. 260)
venomous, tantrum, chloroform, mania, bootlegger, euphemism (p. 261)
conspicuous, prodigious (p. 262)
pathos, cynical, solitary (p. 265)
amiable, agitation, prim, monotony (p. 267)
polecat (pp. 272, 282), *weltschmerzlich* (p. 269)
vexed, infamous, haberdashery (p. 270)
pilfers, concentrated, mite (p. 271)
stupendous, wrenching, perishing (p. 272)
Methuselah, mesmerized (p. 273)
insouciant (p. 275)
desultory (p. 276)
deliberative, floorwaker (p. 277)
mottled, vexation, pandemonium, giddy, condescending (p. 278)
Miss Fagin, enterprise, idiosyncrasy (p. 279)
crucial (p. 280)
transient, afflicted (p. 281)
curmudgeon, declamation, nurtured, hemlocks, prig (p. 282)

PASSAGE MASTER

Two passages that contrast the nature of the relationship between Emily and Lottie are (1) when they first meet in her home to steal a cake (pp. 263-263) and (2) when Emily betrays Lottie in Woolworth's (pp. 279-280).

My students respond to these passages when they hear them as Reader's Theater—when parts have been assigned and read as a radio script. As a follow up, I always have the students discuss or write a journal on who gave the most dramatic and convincing performance. In other words, which character's emotional expression was more convincing.

CONNECTOR

The Connector's contribution to discussion is to write and raise at least four evaluation questions—two about personal experience and two about personal values. Suggestions:

1. Have you ever stolen anything of value? Why? How did you feel? Did you get caught? If not, did you continue to steal? (values)

2. Have you ever been caught stealing or doing something else illegal? If so, how did you feel? What did you say? What did you do? (experience)

3. Have you ever had a friend who you discovered was doing something wrong? If so, what did you do? How did you react? (experience)

4. What is worse than stealing? Why? What is not as bad as stealing? Why? (values)

"Two Soldiers"

Lesson Plan 10

1. Focus:

What is your definition of patriotism? What is the difference between a genuine and phony patriot? (Journal or Response Log)

2. Objective:

♦ To understand the nature and requirements of six role sheets on this novel that participants will share in their small-group discussions.

♦ To review the Three Kinds of Questions and Qualities of Good Discussion Questions.

3. Purpose:

To prepare students for small-group discussion.

4. Input and Modeling:

Plot-check Quiz on Three Kinds of Questions and Exercise on the Qualities of Good Questions on the short story by William Faulkner.

5. Checking for Understanding:

Review the Plot-Check Quiz and the Exercise on Qualities of Good Questions.

6. Guided Practice:

Review the content of each of the six role sheets: Discussion Coleaders, Characters Captain, Passage Master, Connector, and Movie Critic.

7. Closure:

Extol good examples and make suggestions for those that need improvement.

Source: Faulkner, W. (1950). Two soldiers. *Collected Stories of William Faulkner* (pp. 81-99). New York: Random House.

Film: "Two Soldiers" The American Film Institute. VHS 30 min. Monterey Home Video, Director, Christopher Lula.

Internet: Web master John Padgett, professor of English at Ole Miss, boldly asserts that this is "the most extensive site on Faulkner in the world." http://www.mcsr.olemiss.edu/%7Eegjbp/faulkner/faulkner.html

"TWO SOLDIERS"

PLOT-CHECK QUIZ
HANDOUT

Directions: Choose the best answer by marking the scantron. Please do not mark on this test.

1. "Me and Pete," the first three words of the story, refers to:
    a. Billy Joe and his brother
    b. The narrator and his cousin
    c. The narrator and his brother

2. The narrator of the story is almost ___ years old.
    a. Nine
    b. Ten
    c. Fifteen
    d. Seventeen
    e. Twenty

3. Pete is almost ___ years old.
    a. Nine
    b. Ten
    c. Fifteen
    d. Seventeen
    e. Twenty

4. The story takes place in (two answers):
    a. Memphis
    b. Oxford
    c. Frenchman's Bend
    d. Mississippi
    e. Jefferson

5. The time of the story is during the _____ World War.
    a. First
    b. Second
    c. Civil
    d. Revolutionary

6. Pete goes to the city because he had been drafted:
    a. True
    b. False

7. When Pete left home, he was most concerned about the effect his absence would have on his:
   a. Maw
   b. Pap
   c. brother
   d. sister
   e. None of these

8. Pete's mother is *against* his leaving home because she:
   a. can't think of one good reason.
   b. thinks that her brother did enough in WW I
   c. knows he will get into trouble.
   d. thinks his brother will want to leave home next
   e. None of these.

9. Pete's father is *against* his leaving home because:
   a. He had done enough already.
   b. He needed Pete's help on the farm.
   c. He had gotten into trouble himself.
   d. He agreed with Pete's mother's thinking.
   e. None of these.

10. Pete's brother is both *for and against* his brother's leaving home.
    a. True
    b. False.

11. Since Pete felt that he had to leave home, that he's "got to go," his brother assumed that he would have to go with him.
    a. True
    b. False

12. Pete never did give a reason for leaving home.
    a. True
    b. False

13. The author wants us to admire Pete's reason for leaving home.
    a. True
    b. False

14. The author wants us to think that Pete's brother is foolish for wanting to leave home with his brother.
    a. True
    b. False

15. Pete's brother finally gets to the city where Pete had gone by:
    a. Walking
    b. Walking and a bus
    c. Hitchhiking
    d. Bus
    e. Train

16. When the narrator finally gets to Memphis and finds his brother, Pete is:
    a. Curious
    b. Astonished
    c. Disgusted
    d. Angry
    e. Embarrassed

17. Pete immediately reprimands his brother for:
    a. Using profane language
    b. Using his knife
    c. Whining and whimpering
    d. Disobeying him
    e. Not telling his parents he had also left home

18. Peter's brother told him that he had come to Memphis because:
    a. He wanted to say good-bye
    b. His heart hurt
    c. He knew he wanted him to come
    d. He knew he would need wood and water
    e. None of these

19. Pete's brother is astonished when his older brother:
    a. Hits him on the head
    b. Takes away his knife
    c. Kisses him
    d. Shouts angrily at him
    e. Tells him the Army had rejected him

20. When Pete's brother returns home, he:
    a. Tells his parents he's sorry for being so late
    b. Begins crying uncontrollably
    c. Tells his parents he wanted to see Pete
    d. Blames Pete for leaving home
    e. None of these

ANSWER KEY

1.	c	6.	b	11.	a	16.	b
2.	a	7.	c	12.	a	17.	d
3.	e	8.	a	13.	a	18.	b
4.	a & c	9.	b	14.	b	19.	c
5.	b	10.	a	15.	c	20.	b

"TWO SOLDIERS"

REVIEW QUIZ ON QUALITIES OF GOOD QUESTIONS HANDOUT

Directions: On your own paper, mark GOOD if a question would lead to a disagreement based on the story. If the question lacks one of the needed qualities, mark it:

NC if the question is NOT CLEAR and would have to be explained.
NS if the question is NOT SPECIFIC and could be asked of any story.
LD for LACKS DOUBT since it cannot be answered in more than one way.
FACT for FACTUAL and cannot be discussed.
EVAL for EVALUATION and not about understanding the story.

_____ 1.   Does Pete really love his little brother?

_____ 2.   Why does Pete's younger brother look up to his older brother?

_____ 3.   What's wrong with Pete's little brother?

_____ 4.   What kind of relationship do Pete and his brother have?

_____ 5.   Does the title, "Two Soldiers" imply anything more than patriotism?

_____ 6.   Why doesn't Pete's brother understand why he cannot go to war with Pete?

_____ 7.   How important is your relationship with your brother(s) and sister(s)?

_____ 8.   Why is Pete's little brother nameless in Faulkner's story?

_____ 9.   Is the author using Pete?

_____ 10.   Why is Pete's little brother so determined to see his brother in Memphis.

ANSWER KEY

REVIEW QUIZ ON QUALITIES OF GOOD QUESTIONS

1. Does Pete really love his little brother?

    LD: Of course. There is no evidence that would make a us doubt it.

2. Why does Pete's younger brother look up to his older brother?

    GOOD interpretive question.

3. What's wrong with Pete's little brother?

    NC: Not clear. What does "wrong" mean here?

4. What kind of relationship do Pete and his brother have?

    NS: Can be asked of any two characters in any story.

5. Does the title, "Two Soldiers" imply anything more than patriotism?

    GOOD interpretive question.

6. Why doesn't Pete's brother understand why he cannot go to war with Pete?

    LD: No. He's too young to understand and refuses to take no.

7. How important is your relationship with your brother(s) and sister(s)?

    EVAL: A question about personal values.

8. Why is Pete's little brother nameless in Faulkner's story?

    GOOD interpretive question.

9. Is the author using Pete?

    NC: Not clear. What does "using" mean?

10. Why is Pete's little brother so determined to see his brother in Memphis"

    GOOD interpretive question

SUGGESTIONS FOR SIX ROLE SHEETS: CAVEAT

The suggestions for these six role sheets are only that, suggestions. They are NOT to be given to the students since that would defeat a major purpose of Literature Circles. According to Principal 6, "Discussion questions [and other ideas in the role sheets] come from the students, not from teachers or text-books."

Then why offer these ideas at all? Only to give teachers models of good questions and suggestions that they may sometimes need to come up with when they have a mental block or when they are at a loss for ideas to help their students. In short, these suggestions serve their purpose best when they become a catalyst for a teacher's own ideas and models for their students during mini-lessons before or after discussion.

COLEADERS DISCUSSION QUESTIONS: PREPARED QUESTIONS

1. Why is the story told from the view point of Pete's 9-year-old brother?

2. Why does Faulkner have his narrator speak in dialect?

3. Why does Pete never explain why he *has* to go to war?

4. Why doesn't Pete's mother understand why Pete *has* to go to war?

5. Does Faulkner want us to regard Pete's father as unpatriotic because he can see no use in his son joining the U.S. Army?

6. Why does Pete's brother hold back his tears when Pete gets on the bus to Memphis (p. 88) but cry uncontrollably when the soldier drives him home to Frenchman's bend? (p. 99) (Note to the teacher: you may want to bring up this question *after* the class has written their resolutions to the story).

7. Why does Faulkner contrast the poverty of the Grier family with the wealth of the Colonel, his wife, and son?

8. Why does the movie version omit the scene where Mrs. McKellogg takes Pete's brother to her home for dinner?

9. Why does the movie change Faulkner's ending to the story?

10. Why would Faulkner have rejected the movie's ending of his story?

CHARACTERS CAPTAIN

- ◆ Setting: Frenchman's Bend, Mississippi and Memphis, Tennesse, 1941 (Pearl Harbor)

- ◆ Mr. Grier: Pete's father cannot "see a bit of use" in Pete going to war. The United States has not been invaded and he needs Pete's help to keep up with farm work.

- ◆ Mrs. Grief: Pete's decision to go to war deeply upsets her because it reminds her of how upset her mother was when her brother Marsh went off to WW I. "Just don't ask me to understand why" Pete has also got to go to war.

- ◆ Pete Grier: After Pete (19) hears about the attack on Pearl Harbor followed by an appeal for more men to join the Army, he realizes "I got to go."

- ◆ Pete's brother: The 9-year-old narrator who is nameless in Faulkner's story but called Evan in the film version. He is unable to understand why he cannot go to war with Pete: "If you got to go, then so have I."

- ◆ Old Man Killegrew: The Grier family's neighbor whose radio is Pete's source of information on the progress of the war.

- ◆ Mr. Foote: The Sheriff, "the Law," who takes Pete's brother to the bus depot because he believes that he is a runaway; he calls Mrs. Habersham, a social worker, for help.

- ◆ Colonel McKellogg: At the Army depot, he intervenes when Pete's brother knifes a soldier registrar who tried to grab him.

- ◆ Mrs. McKellogg: The Colonel's wife befriends Pete's brother because he reminds her of her son who is near the same age. She takes him to her home for a meal before while Pete's brother is waiting to return to Frenchman's Bend.

WORDSMITH

Since the story is told by a 9-year-old narrator, Pete's brother, Faulkner has him speak with a farm boy's dialect, carefully selecting his simple vocabulary. As a result, the only words that would be unfamiliar to today's students are archaic: vetch, vittles, grip—none of which is hinders the meaning of the story.

PASSAGE MASTER

The evident choice here is when Pete and his brother finally meet at the Army depot in Memphis (pp. 95-97). Begin at: "Then the first soldier opened the door and Pete come in" and end with: "It was a piece of chewing gum."

My students respond to this passage when they hear it as Reader's Theater—when parts have been assigned and read as a radio script. As a follow up, I always have the students discuss or write a journal (or response log) on who gave the most dramatic and convincing performance. In other words, which reader's emotional expression was more convincing.

CONNECTOR

The Connector's contribution to discussion is to write and raise at least four evaluation questions—two about personal experience and two about personal values. Suggestions:

1. Why and when do younger brothers (sisters) look up to their older brothers (sisters)?
2. How important is your relationship with your brother(s) and sister(s)?
3. If you have no brothers or sisters, do you ever wish that had one?
4. Why are some brothers (sisters) very close—even best friends, while others are not?

MOVIE CRITIC

Note: Write your own resolution to the story. You must have noticed that "Two Soldiers" stops; it does not end. The last paragraph has been omitted; it has no resolution.

♦ Begin by listing any question(s) about the story that seem unanswered. In other words, what do you still want to know about Pete's little brother?

♦ Reread the last page beginning with the sentence, "She had a car." Make notations on your story about the way the boy tells his story. What is distinctive about the way Pete's little brother speaks?

♦ Write your own resolution for hand in. Anticipate how you think Faulkner ended his story. Your resolution must imitate the style and tone of its 9-year-old narrator. You are NOT merely describing a conclusion

BUT writing it as though you were Faulkner writing the last paragraph of his story.

♦ Write a one-page essay about the film's resolution. Begin with a topic sentence (thesis) that describes the difference between the movie and story's resolution. State AND explain two or three reasons Faulkner would not have approved this ending.

♦ Model topic sentence (thesis): Unlike Faulkner's "Two Soldiers," which ends with Pete's brother in tears, the movie ends with him telling his parents that he is sorry he is so late. Faulkner would have rejected this conclusion to his story for several reasons.

"Two Soldiers"

The Author's Resolution: The Final Paragraph
William Faulkner

Then we was gone again. And now I could see Memphis good, bright in the sunshine, while we was swinging around it. And the first thing I knowed, we was back on the same highway the bus run on this morning—the patches of stores and them big gins and sawmills, and Memphis running on for miles, it seemed like to me, before it begun to give out. Then we was running again between the fields and woods, running fast now, and except for that soldier, it was like I hadn't never been to Memphis a-tall. We was going fast now. At this rate, before I knowed it we would be home again, and I thought about me riding up to Frenchman's Bend in this big car with a soldier running it, and all of a sudden I begun to cry. I never knowed I was fixing to, and I couldn't stop it. I set there by that soldier, crying. We was going fast.

"THE TWO BROTHERS"
LESSON PLAN 11

1. Focus:

What is your definition of happiness? (Journal or Response Log) For other options, see Connector's worksheet.

2. Objective:

♦ To understand the nature and requirements of six role sheets on this novel that participants will share in their small-group discussions.

♦ To review the Three Kinds of Questions and Qualities of Good Discussion Questions.

3. Purpose:

To prepare students for small-group discussion.

4. Input and Modeling:

Plot-Check Quiz on Three Kinds of Questions and Exercise on the Qualities of Good Questions on the fable by Leo Tolstoy, "The Two Brothers."

5. Checking for Understanding:

Review the Plot-Check Quiz and the Exercise on Qualities of Good Questions.

6. Guided Practice:

Review the content of each of the six role sheets: Discussion Coleaders, Characters Captain, Passage Master, and Connector.

7. Closure:

Extol good examples and make suggestions for those that need improvement.

Sources: Tolstoy, L. (2002). *Classic tales and fables for children.* Amherst, NY: Prometheus Books.

Internet: http://en.wikipedia.org/wiki/Tolstoy
http://en.wikiquote.org/wiki/Leo_Tolstoy

"The Two Brothers"

Leo Tolstoy

1 Two brothers set out on a journey together. At noon they lay down in a forest to rest. When they woke up they saw a stone lying next to them. There was something written on the stone, and they tried to make out what it was.

2 "Whoever finds this stone," they read, "let him go straight into the forest at sunrise. In the forest a river will appear; let him swim across the river to the other side. There he will find a she-bear and her cubs. Let him take the cubs from her and run up the mountain with them, without once looking back. On top of the mountain he will see a house, and in that house he will find happiness."

3 When they had read what was written on the stone, the younger brother said: "Let us go together. We can swim across the river, carry off the bear cubs, take them to the house on the mountain, and together find happiness."

4 "I am not going into the forest after bear cubs," said the elder brother, "and I advise you not to go. In the first place, no one can know whether what is written on this stone is the truth—perhaps it was written in jest. It is even possible that we have not read it correctly. In the second place, even if what is written here is the truth—suppose we go into the forest and night comes, and we cannot find the river. We shall be lost. And if we do find the river, how are we going to swim across it? It may be broad and swift. In the third place, even if we swim across the river, do you think it is an easy thing to take her cubs away from a she-bear? She will seize us, and instead of finding happiness, we shall perish, and all for nothing. In the fourth place, even if we succeeded in carrying off the bear cubs, we could not run up a mountain without stopping to rest. And, most important of all, the stone does not tell us what kind of happiness we should find in that house. It may be that happiness awaiting us there is not at all the sort of happiness we would want."

5 "In my opinion," said the younger brother, "you are wrong. What is written on the stone could not have been put there without reason. And it is all perfectly clear. In the first place, no harm will come to us if we try. In the second place, if we do not go, someone else will read the inscription on the stone and find happiness, and we shall have lost it all. In the third place, if you do not make an effort and try hard, nothing in the world will succeed. In the fourth place, I should not want it thought that I was afraid of anything."

6 The elder brother answered him by saying: "The proverb says: 'In seeking great happiness small pleasures may be lost.' And also: 'A bird in the hand is worth two in the bush.'"

7 The younger brother replied: "I have heard: 'He who is afraid of the leaves must not go into the forest.' And also: 'Beneath a stone no water flows.'" "Then the younger brother set off, and the elder remained behind.

8 No sooner had the younger brother gone into the forest than he found the river, swam across it, and there on the other side was the she-bear, fast asleep. He took her cubs, and ran up the mountain without looking back. When he reached the top of the mountain the people came out to meet him with a carriage to take him into the city, where they made him their king.

9 He ruled for five years. In the sixth year, another king, who was stronger than he, waged war against him. The city was conquered, and he was driven out.

10 Again the younger brother became a wanderer, and he arrived one day at the house of the elder brother. The elder brother was living in a village and had grown neither rich nor poor. The two brothers rejoiced at seeing each other and at once began telling of all that had happened to them.

11 "You see," said the elder brother, "I was right. Here I have lived quietly and well, while you, though you may have been a king, have seen a great deal of trouble." "I do not regret having gone into the forest and up the mountain," replied the younger brother. "I may have nothing now, but I shall always have something to remember, while you have no memories at all."

"The Two Brothers"

Plot-check Quiz
Handout

Directions: On your own paper, answer each question briefly in the space beneath it and then identify the type of each question: print FACT for factual, INT for interpretation, and EVAL for evaluation.

____   1.   What do the brothers have to do to find happiness?

____   2.   What kind of happiness is the elder brother looking for?

____   3.   What is happiness?

____   4.   Is the younger brother confident that he found happiness?

____   5.   Does the younger brother want to find happiness with his older brother?

____   6.   Why are both brothers happy with their own lives?

____   7.   How do the brothers react when they met each other years later?

____   8.   Why does Tolstoy conclude by giving the younger brother the last word?

____   9.   Could the story have been concluded in a better way?

____10.   Does Tolstoy want us to think that the younger brother made the better choice?

ANSWER KEY

PLOT-CHECK QUIZ

1. What do the brothers have to do to find happiness?

   FACT: They are to follow the directions on the stone (para. 2).

2. What kind of happiness is the elder brother looking for?

   INT: Good question for discussion that has different correct answers depending on the supporting evidence. (para. 4 and 11)

3. What is happiness?

   EVAL: A question about personal values.

4. Is the younger brother confident that he found happiness?

   FACT: Yes. He has many good memories. (para. 11)

5. Does the younger brother want to find happiness with his older brother?

   FACT: Yes. He invites his older brother to go with him. (para. 3)

6. Why are both brothers happy with their own lives?

   FACT: The elder brother says he lived "quietly and well" while the younger has no regrets because he has good memories. (para. 11)

7. How do the brothers react when they met each other years later?

   FACT: They rejoiced and immediately began relating everything that had happened to them when they were apart. (para. 10)

8. Why does Tolstoy conclude by giving the younger brother the last word?

   INT: Good question for discussion that has different correct answers depending on the supporting evidence.

9. Could the story have been concluded in a better way?

   EVAL: A question about personal values.

10. Does Tolstoy want us to think that the younger brother made the better choice?

    INT: A good basic question of interpretation that involves the entire story.

"Two Brothers"

Review Quiz on Qualities of Good Questions Handout

Directions: On your own paper, mark GOOD if a question would lead to a disagreement based on the story. If the question lacks one of the needed qualities, mark it:

NC if the question is NOT CLEAR and would have to be explained.
NS if the question is NOT SPECIFIC and could be asked of any story.
LD for LACKS DOUBT since it cannot be answered in more than one way.
FACT for FACTUAL and cannot be discussed.
EVAL for EVALUATION and not about understanding the story.

_____ 1. Are both brothers certain about their ideas of happiness?

_____ 2. Why were the two brothers invited to make a journey?

_____ 3. According to the story, is taking risks necessary to find happiness?

_____ 4. What kind of relationship is there between the two brothers?

_____ 5. Is the happiness that the brothers experience left vague on purpose?

_____ 6. Would you have followed the writing on the stone?

_____ 7. Does Tolstoy portray the older brother as a stick in the mud?

_____ 8. Why does the younger brother believe the message on the stone while the elder brother mistrusts it?

_____ 9. Why does the younger brother assume that his older brother will have "no memories at all" of his past life?

_____ 10. How do the two brothers get along in the years after their reunion?

_____ 11. What is the narrator trying to imply in this story?

_____ 12. Why is each brother happy with his own life?

ANSWER KEY

REVIEW QUIZ ON QUALITIES OF GOOD QUESTIONS

1. Are both brothers certain about their ideas of happiness?

   LD: Yes. There is no evidence that either brother is doubtful.

2. Why were the two brothers invited to make a journey?

   FACT: To find happiness.

3. According to the story, is taking risks necessary to find happiness?

   GOOD interpretive question for discussion.

4. What kind of relationship is there between the two brothers?

   NS: This question can be asked of any two characters in any story. It is not enough of a problem of interpretation. See question 9 for a specific question about their relationship.

5. Is the happiness that the brothers experience left vague on purpose?

   NC: What happiness did they leave?

6. Would you have followed the writing on the stone?

   EVAL: A question about personal values.

7. Does Tolstoy portray the older brother as a stick in the mud?

   NC: Not clear. What does "stick in the mud mean"? Avoid colloquialisms.

8. Why does the younger brother believe the message on the stone while the elder brother mistrusts it?

   FACT: Each brother explains in detail his reasons for not going (para. 4) and for following the stone's directions (para. 5).

9. Why does the younger brother assume that his older brother will have "no memories at all" of his past life?

   GOOD interpretive question for discussion.

10. How do the two brothers get along in the years after their reunion?

    NA: Not answerable. Any answer would be mere speculation.

11. What is the narrator trying to imply in this story?

    NS: Not a specific problem of interpretation. Where do you want us to begin in the story?

12. Why is each brother happy with his own life?

    GOOD interpretive question for discussion.

SUGGESTIONS FOR SIX ROLE SHEETS: CAVEAT

The suggestions for these six role sheets are only that, suggestions. They are NOT to be given to the students since that would be defeat the a major purpose of Literature Circles. According to Principal 6, "Discussion questions [and other ideas in the role sheets] come from the students, not from teachers or textbooks."

Then why offer these ideas at all? So as only to give teachers models of good questions and suggestions that they may sometimes need to come up with when they have a mental block or when they are at a loss for ideas to help their students. In short, these suggestions serve their purpose best when they become a catalyst for a teacher's own ideas and models for their students during mini-lessons before or after discussion.

COLEADER DISCUSSION QUESTIONS: PREPARED QUESTIONS

According to Tolstoy, does the younger or older brother make the better choice?

1. Why does the younger brother want to follow the stone's directions together with his older brother rather than alone? (para. 3)
2. What "sort of happiness" is the older brother looking for? (para. 4)
3. Are the younger or the older brother's arguments meant to be more convincing? (para. 3 and 7)
4. Why doesn't the younger brother answer each of his older brother's arguments for rejecting the stone's directions? (para. 5)
5. How do the two proverbs quoted by the elder brother rebut the younger brother's arguments? (para. 6)
6. How do the two proverbs quoted by the younger brother rebut his brother's proverbs? (para. 7)
7. Why doesn't the younger brother find happiness "in a house" as written on the stone? (para. 2)
8. Why does Tolstoy have the younger brother overthrown as a king while the older brother became "neither rich nor poor"? (para. 9 and 10)
9. Why does the story end with both brothers happy?
10. Why does Tolstoy give the younger brother the last word?

11. Why does the younger brother assume that his older brother has no memories of his past life? (para. 11)

12. Does Tolstoy imply that taking risks is necessary to be happy?

13. Does Tolstoy imply that happiness is a goal in itself or the result of pursuing other goals?

Characters Captain

♦ Setting: "Once upon a time …"

♦ Elder brother: "Most important of all, the stone does not tell us what kind of happiness we should find in that house. It may be that happiness awaiting us there is not the sort we would want."

♦ Younger brother: "You are wrong … If you do not make an effort and try hard, nothing in the world will succeed …. 'He who is afraid of leaves must not go into the forest.' "

Passage Master

Since the story is but one page, I always do the first reading as a Reader's Theater.

Connector

(Journal or Response Log)

TIME magazine (January 17, 2005) devoted most of the issue to a discussion of the nature of happiness. (1) With which of the quotations below would the younger or the older brother agree? Why? (2) With which of these quotations would you agree?

1. "If only we would stop trying to be happy, we would have a pretty good time."

—Edith Wharton

2. "People are about as happy as they make up their minds to be happy."

—Abraham Lincoln

3. "Happiness consists more in small conveniences or pleasures that occur every day, than in great pieces of good fortune that happen but seldom to a man in the course of his life."

—Ben Franklin

4. "Striving for happiness is as futile as trying to increase your height."
—Mark Twain

5. "We hold these truths to be self-evident—that all men are created equal endowed by their Creator with certain inalienable rights, that among these are life, liberty, and the pursuit of happiness."

—Thomas Jefferson

6. "Happiness is not a destination but a journey."

—Robert Frost

7. "Happiness consists not in how far we go but in the direction we take."
—Anonymous

8. "I chose the road less traveled and that has made all the difference."
—"The Road Not Taken"

Nonfiction Followup Readings

♦ Had Pete read Lorri-Ann's perceptive essay for her senior English class, "The Futility of High School Romance," he may not have ruined his relationship with Sucker. At least he may have realized that Maybelle did him a favor by dumping him. (Source: http://www.planetpapers.com/Assets/3924.php)

♦ Does Lottie Jump shoplift only because she is poor? While that may be one reason, a study by the Sacramento County Sheriff's department, "Why do people shoplift? concludes that motivations vary as much as individuals and circumstances. (Source: http://www.sacsheriff.com/index.cfm)

♦ Faulkner's *"Two Soldiers"* raises the question about the nature of true patriotism. A Forum of *The Nation* magazine (July 15, 1991), "What is Patriotism" offers a collection of half-page answers, paragraphs, that could easily be edited as a class reading. These answers by politicians, historians, and journalists are certain to provoke strong reactions among your students—negative as well as positive. (Source: http://www.thenation.com/doc/19910715/forum)

♦ In her essay "On Happiness," Jill Carattini compares and contrasts the views of materialist Sigmund Freud and Christian apologist C.S. Lewis. Would either of the two brothers in Tolstoy's fable agree with Freud or Lewis's concept of happiness? If so, why? If not, why not? (Source: http://www.rzim.org/slicetran.php?sliceid=820)

7

How Do True Leaders Inspire Followers While False Leaders Deceive?

Although George Orwell's, *Animal Farm*, is commonly regarded as a satire and critique of the modern totalitarian state, it can also be viewed a fascinating animal story, a fable, or, as Orwell himself called it, a fairy story. In short, it can be regarded as the failure of leadership or how an intelligent, devoted leader of the revolution to better the miserable lives of animals on Manor Farm, Snowball, is driven out by a Napoleon that some animals think is "always right." This basic question comes readily to mind: How is Napoleon able to brand Snowball a traitor when he is acclaimed Hero First Class for having masterminded the defeat of Farmer Jones' attempt to take back Manor Farm?

The brilliant Hallmark movie version (1999), although basically faithful to the original story, makes a colossal plot change that Orwell would have surely rejected because it contradicts entirely his major theme that power corrupts. The movie's narrator is Jessie (a minor character in Orwell's story) who immediately evokes our sympathy for the exploited animals by being so personally involved in their sufferings. However, she not only tells the story but adds her own commentary and interpretation of events. In the prologue, she says "The poisonous cement which once held Napoleon's evil dream together was being washed away … I was blind but I could still remember." She then tells Orwell's story in retrospect and remains basically true to it. But her epilogue is filled with hope: "After all we'd been through, I needed to believe there was still hope … What of the future? There are new owners. We will not allow them to make the same mistakes." The basic question now is, of course, Unlike Orwell's grim resolution, why does the screen writer end the story with Jessie's belief that the Animal Farm can be rebuilt?

Although Orwell's story can be taken at face value, it is not only a fairy tale but also "An Allegory of Communism" that illustrates "the moral bankruptcy of Russian Communism." After providing some background on the history of the former Soviet Union, ask your students which characters in the novel and the film represent (1) Lenin, (2) Stalin, (3) Trotsky, (4) the tsar, and which sets of animals are (5) the secret police and which are (6) the Communist party.

The Lion, The Witch, and the Wardrobe of C. S. Lewis can also be viewed as the confrontation between true and false leadership—that is between Aslan, creator and king of Narnia, and the White Witch who has cast the country into perpetual winter. Early in the story, after the White Witch tricks Edmund into betraying his brother Peter and his sisters, Susan and Lucy, the story becomes a continuing complicated conflict between the army of Jadis and the forces of Narnians loyal to Aslan. In their final apocalyptic battle, Aslan overcomes the evil White Witch. The basic question then becomes, "why do Aslan's followers never lose faith in his leadership while the followers of the White Witch abandoned her?"

If C. S. Lewis had lived to see the movie version of Disney and Walden Media (2005), he would surely would have enthusiastically endorsed it for its spectacular special effects, superb cast, moments of humor, and mix of evil and humanity at its best. According to one of his biographers, Walter Hooper (*Complete Guide to the Life and Works of C. S. Lewis*, 1996), Lewis adamantly refused to allow any of the *Chronicles of Narnia* to be made into movies. His great concern was that his stories would be trivialized as Hollywood cartoons. When Mark Johnson, producer and Andrew Adamson, director, finally secured permission from Douglas Gresham, Lewis' stepson, they had to agree to one condition— that they would remain entirely faithful to the original story. They readily accepted. Nevertheless, they did make, with permission, several minor but significant plot changes that raise several discussion questions.

Although C. S. Lewis readily admits that his story stands on its own and can be understood and enjoyed by anyone, he does also say, "Aslan is an invention giving an imaginary answer to the question, 'What might Christ become like if there really were a world like Narnia and He chose to be incarnate and die and rise again in that world as He actually has done in ours?' " In other words, *The Chronicles of Narnia* are more *suppositions* than allegories which are point-by-point representations of historic events like *Gulliver's Travels* or *Animal Farm*. "Is Aslan a Christ Figure?" illustrates the difference of opinion between those who think that Lewis's choice of Aslan (the Turkish word for lion) is entirely appropriate while others regard it as inconsistent with the Jesus of the Gospel

Animal Farm

Lesson Plan 12

1. Focus:
When did you need your family most? (Journal or Response Log)

2. Objective:
♦ To understand the nature and requirements of six role sheets on this short story that participants will share in their small-group discussions.

♦ To review the Three Kinds of Questions and Qualities of Good Discussion Questions.

3. Purpose:
To prepare students for small-group discussion.

4. Input and Modeling:
Plot-Check Quiz on Three Kinds of Questions and Exercise on the Qualities of Good Questions on Orwell's novel.

5. Checking for Understanding:
Review the Plot-Check Quiz and the Exercise on Qualities of Good Questions.

6. Guided Practice:
Review the content of each of the six role sheets: Discussion Coleaders, Characters Captain, Passage Master, Wordsmith, Connector, and Movie Critic.

7. Closure:
Extol good examples and make suggestions for those that need improvement.

Source: Orwell, G. (1954). *Animal farm*. New York: Harcourt Brace.

Film: *Animal Farm*. Hallmark Home Entertainment. 1999. Color VHS 95 min. *Animal Farm*. Digiview Productions. Animation. 2004 DVD 75 min.

Internet: http://students.ou.edu/C/Kara.C.Chiodo-1/orwell.html

ANIMAL FARM
PLOT-CHECK QUIZ
HANDOUT

Directions: (1) On your own paper, match each name or event with its description (1-15). (2) Answer each question briefly (16-30) and then identify the type of question at the left: print FACT for factual, INT for interpretation, and EVAL for evaluation.

Old Major	Mollie	Boxer	Mr. Pilkington
Moses	Squealer	Napoleon	Battle of the Cowshed
Clover	Snowball	Mr. Whymper	Battle of the Windmill
Muriel	Benjamin	Mr. Frederick	Battle of the Bulge

PART 1

1. He is caught in the barn with a can of white paint just before Muriel noticed that "to excess" had been added to the Fifth Commandment.
2. He has two sayings: "I will work harder" and "Comrade Napoleon is always right."
3. They are decorated "Animal Hero, First Class" at the Battle of the Cowshed.
4. A defector who likes sugar and ribbons more than work, "an enemy of the people."
5. She keeps wanting to know if the Commandments have remained the same.
6. His speech was the inspiration for the Rebellion at Manor Farm.
7. He preaches the gospel of Sugarcandy Mountain which a considerable number of the animals accept as true.
8. He believes that Animal Farm should be returned to its original name, Manor Farm.
9. He remains loyal to Boxer, never laughs, and refuses to take sides in the disputes between Snowball and Napoleon.
10. Mr. Jones and a half dozen men from Foxwood and Pinchfield Farms attempt to retake Manor Farm but fail.
11. He acts as a go-between for business deals between humans and animals.

12. He leads the attack on Animal Farm with 15 armed men that attempt to blow up the windmill.

13. He makes a speech to point out that between pigs and humans there is not and need not be any clash of interests whatsoever.

14. She is a goat who reads for Clover the Commandments on the barn wall.

15. At this time, Napoleon is given the decoration of the "Order of the Green Banner."

PART 2

16. What was the catalyst that spontaneously brought about the revolution?

17. To what single maxim does Snowball reduce the Seven Commandments?

18. Why do two local farmers attack Animal Farm?

19. In their struggle for leadership, what two tactics does Napoleon employ to win out over Snowball?

20. When Animal Farm begins to deteriorate, what solution does Snowball propose?

21. Why is Napoleon at first against the windmill project but then adopts it?

22. Why does Napoleon begin to engage in trade with neighboring farms?

23. After a storm destroys the windmill, how can Napoleon blame Snowball when he is no longer around?

24. What is the result of Napoleon's contract with Mr. Whymper?

25. Why do some of the animals begin turning in themselves as traitors?

26. How does Napoleon get around the Sixth Commandment forbidding killing?

27. How does Napoleon's contract to sell timber with Mr. Frederick fail?

28. When Animal Farm becomes a republic and Napoleon is elected president, why do the pigs welcome the sudden return of Moses?

29. When the condition of Animal Farm becomes as bad as Manor Farm had been previously, what replaces the Seven Commandments?

30. Why does Orwell end his story with the image of the pigs fighting among themselves?

ANSWER KEY

PLOT-CHECK QUIZ

PART 1

1. He is caught in the barn with a can of white paint just before Muriel noticed that "to excess" had been added to the Fifth Commandment.

   Squealer

2. He has two sayings: "I will work harder" and "Comrade Napoleon is always right."

   Boxer

3. They are decorated "Animal Hero, First Class" at the Battle of the Cowshed.

   Snowball and Boxer

4. A defector who likes sugar and ribbons more than work, "an enemy of the people."

   Mollie

5. She keeps wanting to know if the Commandments have remained the same.

   Clover

6. His speech was the inspiration for the Rebellion at Manor Farm.

   Old Major

7. He preaches the gospel of Sugarcandy Mountain which a considerable number of the animals accept as true.

   Moses

8. He believes that Animal Farm should be returned to its original name, Manor Farm.

   Napoleon

9. He remains loyal to Boxer, never laughs, and refuses to take sides in the disputes between Snowball and Napoleon.

   Benjamin

10. Mr. Jones and a half dozen men from Foxwood and Pinchfield Farms attempt to retake Manor Farm but fail.

    Battle of the Cowshed

11. He acts as a go-between for business deals between humans and animals.

    Mr. Whymper

12. He leads the attack on Animal Farm with 15 armed men that attempt to blow up the windmill.

    Mr. Frederick

13. He makes a speech to point out that between pigs and humans there is not and need not be any clash of interests whatsoever.

    Mr. Pilkington

14. She is a goat who reads for Clover the Commandments on the barn wall.

    Muriel

15. At this time, Napoleon is given the decoration of the "Order of the Green Banner."

    Battle of the Windmill

PART 2

16. FACT: What event spontaneously brought about the revolution?

    Mr. Jones is so drunk one night that he failed to feed the animals.

17. FACT: To what single saying does Snowball reduce the Seven Commandments?

    "FOUR LEGS GOOD, TWO LEGS BAD."

18. FACT: Why do two local farmers attack Animal Farm?

    The animals have taken over Manor Farm and renamed it.

19. FACT: In their struggle for leadership, what two things does Napoleon do to overcome Snowball and get rid of him?

    Napoleon threatens him with nine enormous dogs; appropriates for himself Snowball's windmill plan, and makes him a "traitor."

20. FACT: When Animal Farm begins to deteriorate, what does Snowball propose?

    He proposes that the windmill be turned into a dynamo for electricity to run labor-saving power machinery.

21. INT: Why is Napoleon at first against the windmill project but then adopts it?

   He routs Snowball with the dogs, makes him a traitor, and has Squealer explain that he was not really opposed to the windmill because he knew he could blame Snowball if the project failed.

22. INT: Why does Napoleon begin to engage in trade with neighboring farms?

   Animal Farm is no longer able to sustain itself and he wants to solidify his leadership of the farm.

23. INT: After a storm destroys the windmill, how can Napoleon blame Snowball when he is no longer around?

   No one asks for any evidence that Snowball had anything to do with the loss of the windmill. In addition, Napoleon is already so much in control that he can intimidate into silence anyone who would question him.

24. FACT: What is the result of Napoleon's contract with Mr. Whymper?

   The hens revolt when ordered to increase production to 400 eggs a week but ruthlessly suppresses them as traitors and agents of Snowball.

25. INT: Why do some of the animals begin turning in themselves as traitors?

   Some begin denouncing themselves as traitors and agents of Snowball because of the hysteria that the executions have already created. Some animals are also so stupid that they believe, like Boxer, "something must be wrong with ourselves."

26. FACT: How does Napoleon get around the Sixth Commandment forbidding killing?

   He has Squealer revise it to read: "No animal shall kill any other animal *without cause."*

27. FACT: Why does Napoleon's contract to sell timber with Mr. Frederick fail?

   Frederick pays for the lumber with counterfeit money.

28. INT: When Animal Farm becomes a republic and Napoleon is elected president, why do the pigs welcome the sudden return of Moses?

   When Moses returns again, the pigs welcome him with his gospel of Sugarcandy Mountain, because it makes the animals accept their present misery. In addition, since Moses had been Mr. Jones' spy, he could be useful to Napoleon.

29. INT: Near the end of the story, how can all animals now be equal while some are more equal than others?

    This statement is not a paradox but a contradiction: no one can be more equal than another any more than those executed could be more dead than one another. This statement is a good example of what Orwell calls "doublethink" in *1984*—the ability to believe and to maintain two contradictory ideas at the same time.

30. INT: Why does Orwell end his story with the image of the pigs fighting among themselves?

    When the pigs and the humans began fighting among themselves, "The creatures outside looked from pig to man, and from man to pig, and from pig to man again; but already it was impossible to say which was which."

Note: There are no EVALUATION questions.

Animal Farm

Review Quiz on Qualities of Good Discussion Questions Handout

Directions: On your own paper, mark GOOD if a question would lead to a disagreement based on the book. If the question lacks one of the needed qualities, mark it:

NC if the question is NOT CLEAR
NS if the question is NOT SPECIFIC and could be asked of any story.
LD for LACKS DOUBT since it cannot be answered in more than one way.
FACT for FACTUAL and cannot be discussed.
EVAL for EVALUATION that could be answered without reading the story.

_____ 1. What is Orwell's purpose in writing this story?

_____ 2. Why does the revolution at Animal Farm fail?

_____ 3. Why don't Clover and Benjamin tell the other animals the truth?

_____ 4. How does Napoleon get rid of Snowball?

_____ 5. Why does Boxer react they way he does?

_____ 6. What does Old Major's speech mean?

_____ 7. Why did the pigs become the leaders of Animal Farm?

_____ 8. Have you ever been taken in by a clever trick? If so, how did you feel?

_____ 9. Why does Orwell spend so much time on description?

_____ 10. Why do Squealer and Mollie act like a jerks?

_____ 11. Why does Orwell end the story with the statement that some animals are more equal than others?

_____ 12. What is the message of the story?

_____ 13. Why does Boxer become a model for the other animals?

_____ 14. Does Napoleon really care about improving the lives of the animals?

_____ 15. Why does Orwell end the story with an observer being unable to distinguish the pigs from the men and the men from the pigs.

ANSWER KEY

REVIEW QUIZ ON QUALITIES OF GOOD DISCUSSION QUESTIONS

1. NS: Could be asked of any story.

2. GOOD.

3. NC: What truth? Truth about what?

4. FACT: When Napoleon has the dogs attack him, he runs away for his life.

5. NC: What reaction? To what? When? Where?

6. NS: What, specifically, do you want to know the meaning of in his speech?

7. FACT: They assume the leadership because they were the most intelligent.

8. EVALUATION: Personal experience.

9. NS: What description, specifically, do you want to know about?

10. NC: How do they act like "jerks"? What is a jerk?

11. GOOD

12. NS: Could be asked of any story.

13. FACT: He works harder than anyone else and never questions Napoleon's rule.

14. LD: The answer has to be no since there is no evidence to support a yes.

15. GOOD.

SUGGESTIONS FOR SIX ROLE SHEETS:
CAVEAT

The suggestions for these six role sheets are only that, suggestions. They are NOT to be given to the students since that would defeat a major purpose of Literature Circles. According to Principal 6, "Discussion questions [and other ideas in the role sheets] come from the students, not from teachers or text-books."

Then why offer these ideas at all? So as only to give teachers models of good questions and suggestions that they may sometimes need to come up with when they have a mental block or when they are at a loss for ideas to help their students. In short, these suggestions serve their purpose best when they become a catalyst for a teacher's own ideas and models for their students during mini-lessons before or after discussion.

COLEADER DISCUSSION QUESTIONS:
PREPARED QUESTIONS

1. Why do the animals fail to establish their dream of a perfect society in which everyone worked for the good of all?

2. Since the pigs object to Moses' gospel of Sugarcandy Mountain, why do they allow him to stay around? (p. 27)

3. Of the Seven Commandments, why are four of them do-nots (3-6) and three of them (1, 2 and 7) statements? (p. 33)

4. Are the Seven Commandments ranked in order of importance? (p. 33)

5. Why doesn't Benjamin take sides in the struggle between Snowball and Napoleon for leadership? (pp. 37, 55, 83, and 103)

6. When Clover and Benjamin realize that the Commandments are being changed one by one, why don't they tell the other animals? (pp. 69, 55. 88, and 105)

7. Why don't the animals recognize that something is wrong as the Commandments are changed one by one?

8. After witnessing public executions, why does Boxer think there must be "some fault in ourselves" rather than point out that Napoleon broke the Sixth Commandment? (pp. 33, 84)

9. After the first public executions that bring tears to Clover's eyes, why does she still accept Napoleon's leadership? (p. 85)

10. Does her devotion to Boxer make Clover close her eyes to the evil about her?

11. After Animal Farm is proclaimed a republic, and Napoleon elected president, why does Moses suddenly reappear after several years absence? (p. 109)

12. Eventually, why are the animals unable to judge whether or not their condition is worse or better than when they lived under Mr. Jones? (p. 119)

13. Although the Seventh Commandment says "all animals are equal," how does it happen that some pigs become "more equal" than others? (p. 123)

14. Why does the story end with the observation that the animals and the humans are unable to distinguish between themselves? (p. 128)

15. Why does the story end with the name of Animal Farm being changed back to Manor Farm?

CHARACTERS CAPTAIN

MAJOR CHARACTERS

♦ Farmer Jones is the incompetent, selfish, and alcoholic manager of Manor Farm. Unwittingly, he causes the spontaneous rebellion of the animals when he fails to feed them.

♦ Napoleon: When Animal Farm becomes a republic, he is its first president since he is the only candidate. Not as intelligent as his archrival Snowball, he does know how to manipulate Squealer, the dogs, and the pigs into serving his own selfish ends.

♦ Snowball: The most intelligent of the animals, his brilliant defense plan enables the animals to successfully defend against the neighboring farmers attempt to take back Animal Farm. When he becomes Animal Hero First Class, Napoleon promptly turns him into a scapegoat and traitor.

♦ Old Major: Looking back on his long life, he relates his prophetic dream in a persuasive speech that Man is the cause of every animal's suffering. His speech becomes the basis for the Seven Commandments and the principles of Animalism.

♦ Squealer: Napoleon's public relations and press agent whose rationalizations convince some of the animals that "Napoleon is always right," even when he's wrong.

♦ The Dogs: Bluebell, Jessie, and Pincher are three dogs, whose puppies Napoleon takes for "conditioning" to become his Secret Police and enforcers. They intimidate any one who questions Napoleon's rules. In the film, Jessie becomes a major character who not only narrates the story, but also provides a running commentary on what is going on.

♦ Mr. Pilkington of Foxwood: His sole concern is greed. Since he cannot defeat the animals after they drive Jones away, he begins to trade with Napoleon for his own benefit.

♦ Mr. Frederick of Pinchfield: He also trades with Napoleon but is more devious than Pilkington. He gives him counterfeit money for lumber. However, in the film he reprimands Pilkington for his exploitation and abuse of the animals.

MINOR

♦ Mr. Whymper: A lawyer hired by Napoleon to act as an intermediary between the Farm and humans on the "outside." He does not appear in the film version.

♦ Moses: A raven who acts as a pet and spy for Farmer Jones. He preaches the gospel of Sugarcandy Mountain (where animals go when they die) to keep them quiet and accepting of their lot in life.

♦ Benjamin: The cynical donkey who does not believe anything will really improve after the Revolution. He is the oldest animal on the farm who rarely expresses his opinion.

♦ Boxer: He is an enormous draft horse whose motto to his death remains, "Napoleon is always right." He eventually works himself to death because he believes totally in the Revolution and says often, "I will work harder."

♦ Clover: A dim witted mare and hard worker who, like Boxer, is tricked repeatedly by the pigs. She tries to save Boxer when he is taken off to the slaughter house.

♦ Muriel: A white goat, who is able to read somewhat better than most of the animals and reads the Commandments for them.

♦ Mollie: A white hedonistic white mare who likes pleasing humans. Since she has no interest in the Revolution, she soon abandons the Farm for town life.

♦ The Cat: Totally independent and rarely seen, he often votes on both sides of an issue

♦ The Sheep: Entirely mindless, they can only bleat slogans in unanimous chorus supporting Napoleon's policies.

WORDSMITH

Even a cursory reading of Orwell's story reveals his sophisticated vocabulary. In short, he is not writing for children although middle school students readily understand the gist of *Animal Farm*. Nevertheless, a sizable list of words would have to be looked up by most students:

cannibalism (p. 45)
ceremonial (p. 76)
complicity (p. 109)
conciliatory (p. 96)
contemplated (p. 93)
contemptible (p. 98)
controversies (p. 53)
cryptic (pp. 38, 71)
drastic (p. 75)
dynamo (pp. 54, 94, 118)
faction (p. 55)
hullabaloo (p. 96)
ignominious (p. 48)
indignantly (p. 115)
indignation (p. 72)
inspiration (p. 75)
imperishable (p. 120)
irrepressible (p. 46)
knacker (p. 20)
laborious (p. 109)
legend (p. 93)
leisure (p. 112)

lurking (p. 81)
maltreating (p. 29)
meddle (p. 88)
morose (p. 117)
pampering (p. 126)
pension (p. 104)
pretext (p. 51)
prosperity (pp. 20, 120)
reconciled (p. 68)
referred (p. 90)
reverent (p. 61)
superannuated (pp. 105, 117)
taciturn (p. 117)
tactics (p. 62)
treachery (pp. 83, 96)
tyranny (p. 20)
unanimous (p. 31, 109)
uproarious (p. 116)
vague (p. 66)
vengeance (p. 98)
vivacious (p. 25)
voluntary (p. 63)

PASSAGE MASTER

Four key passages readily come to mind because they are central to Orwell's major theme that power corrupts:

1. The Old Major's speech (p. 19): "Man is the only creature that consumes without producing ... what have you ever had except your bare rations and a stall?"

2. Napoleon's speech (pp. 58-59): "Napoleon, with the dogs following him, now mounted on the raised portion of the floor where Major had previously stood to deliver his speech ... but there would be no more debates."

3. Clover's interior monologue (pp. 85-86): "As Clover looked down the hillside, her eyes filled with tears. If she could have spoken her thoughts, it would have been to say.— Such were her thoughts, though she lacked the words to express them."

4. The resolution of the story (p. 128): "There was the same hearty cheering as before.... The creatures outside looked from pig to man, and from man to pig, and from pig to man again; but already it was impossible to say which was which."

CONNECTOR

Here are four related questions of evaluation, two about common experience and two about personal values:

1. Is there any one in your life who is your leader? If so, who is it? Why? How do you follow this leader?

2. If you have no leader in your life, can you explain why?

3. How does a phony leader tip his or her hand?

4. Do you know any phony leaders?

FILM NOTES ON *ANIMAL FARM*
VHS (1999) 90 min.

The brilliant Hallmark movie version (1999), although basically faithful to the original story, makes a colossal plot change that Orwell would have surely rejected because it contradicts entirely his major theme that power corrupts. The movie's narrator is Jessie (a minor character in Orwell's story) who immediately evokes our sympathy for the exploited animals by being so personally involved in their sufferings. However, she not only tells the story but adds her own commentary and interpretation of events. In the prologue, she says "The poisonous cement which once held Napoleon's evil dream together was being washed away ... I was blind but I could still remember." She then tells Orwell's story in retrospect and remains basically true to it. But her epilogue is filled with hope: "After all we'd been through, I needed to believe there was still hope ... What of the future? There are new owners. We will not allow them to make the same mistakes." The basic question now is, of course, unlike Orwell's grim resolution, why does the screenwriter end the story with Jessie's belief that the Animal Farm can be rebuilt?

PROLOGUE
by Jessie (Julia Ormond), the Narrator

"It was a storm of judgment. For years we'd been hiding from oppression, hiding from Napoleon's spies. But now nature was washing away the disease. I always knew as with all things built on wrong foundations, the Farm would one day crumble. At last, the wait was over. The poisonous cement which once held Napoleon's evil dream together was being washed away. I could taste it in the water. I was old. I was almost blind but I could still remember."

ANIMAL FARM
Jessie's Epilogue

"Free? Life had been far from free in our hideout. Seasons came and went and we waited. We grew old but we still waited for what surely must pass. Waited for Napoleon's fall. And now with the coming of the storm, came the first signs our wait was over. It was time for us to return to that place that had once been full of such hope. I wondered if anything was still left alive. I knew in my heart that Napoleon had fallen a victim of his own madness. But what of the others? After all we'd been through, I needed to believe there was still hope. Could this be the same place?! All that was left was a memory. My heart sank. But there are always survivors. [Sunshine appears on spring's fields and new puppies bound toward Jessie.] The walls have now fallen. The scars have healed, and life goes on. And what of the future? There are new owners. We will not allow them to make the same mistakes. We will rebuild the farm. And now at last, we shall be free!"

MOVIE CRITIC

When Jessie tells Orwell's story in retrospect she remains basically true to it. However, in contrast, her epilogue is filled with hope (text above). The basic question on the film is, of course: *Unlike Orwell's grim resolution, why does the screenwriter end the story with Jessie's belief that the Animal Farm can be rebuilt?*

THE LION, THE WITCH AND THE WARDROBE

LESSON PLAN 13

1.	Focus	Are there any leaders in your life? If so, is any one more important than another? Why? How can you tell the difference between a true and a phony leader? (Journal or Response Log)
2.	Objective:	♦ To understand the nature and requirements of six role sheets on this novel that participants will share in their small-group discussions. ♦ To review the Three Kinds of Questions and Qualities of Good Discussion Questions.
3.	Purpose:	To prepare students for small-group discussion.
4.	Input and Modeling:	Plot-Check Quiz on Three Kinds of Questions and Exercise on the Qualities of Good Questions on the novel.
5.	Checking for Understanding:	Review the Plot-Check Quiz and the Exercise on Qualities of Good Questions.
6.	Guided Practice:	Review the content of each of the six role sheets: Characters Captain, Discussion Coleaders, Passage Master, Wordsmith, Movie Critic, and Connector.
7.	Closure:	Extol good examples and make suggestions for those that need improvement.

Source: Lewis, C. S. (2002). *The lion, the witch, and the wardrobe.* New York: Harper Collins.

Film: Disney & Walden Media, *The Lion, the Witch, and the Wardrobe.* DVD 2005 135 min.

Internet: www.narnia.com and http://www.imdb.com/title/tt0363771/

THE LION, THE WITCH, AND THE WARDROBE

PLOT-CHECK QUIZ
HANDOUT

Directions: On your own paper, answer each question briefly in the space beneath it and then identify the type of each question: print FACT for factual, INT for interpretation, and EVAL for evaluation.

_____ 1.   Why does Edmund betray his brother and sisters? (pp. 40, 47, and 91)

_____ 2.   Have you ever been tricked into doing something bad?

_____ 3.   Why does Aslan evoke such different feelings in each of the Pevensie children? (p. 74)

_____ 4.   After years of absence, why has Aslan returned to Narnia?

_____ 5.   Why does Aslan inspire fear as well as devotion in his followers? (p. 86)

_____ 6.   Why does Lewis make the White Witch a nonhuman who is "bad all through"? (p. 88)

_____ 7.   Why doesn't Mr. Beaver trust Edmund when he first meets him? (p. 92)

_____ 8.   How do you know when you can trust someone?

_____ 9.   Why does Edmund ridicule a stone lion in the Witch's courtyard?

_____ 10.   When does Edmund conclude that the Queen is evil?

_____ 11.   When with the Witch in her sledge pursuing the children and the Beavers, what happened that for the first time in the story that made Edmund feel sorry for someone besides himself?

_____ 12.   When the children and the Beavers first meet Aslan what does Lucy ask of him?

_____ 13.   Have you every felt guilty about hurting one of your brothers or sisters?

_____ 14.   Why do all the wood people hate the Witch while "her people" obey her every order?

_____ 15.   Why does a lion praise Aslan for his lack of standoffishness? (p. 191)

ANSWER KEY

PLOT-CHECK QUIZ

1. Why does Edmund betray his brother and sisters? (pp. 40, 47, and 91)

   FACT: He believes the Witch's promise of Turkish Delight and adoption (prince).

2. Have you ever been tricked into doing something bad?

   EVAL: A question of personal experience.

3. Why does Aslan evoke such different feelings in each of the Pevensie children? (p. 74)

   INT: A good interpretive question that will evoke differing plausible explanations.

4. After years of absence, why has Aslan returned to Narnia?

   FACT: He has returned to overthrow the Witch. (pp. 74, 84, and 85)

5. Why does Aslan inspire fear as well as devotion in his followers? (p. 86)

   INT: A good interpretive question that will evoke differing plausible explanations.

6. Why does Lewis make the White Witch a nonhuman who is "bad all through"? (p. 88)

   INT: A good interpretive question that will evoke differing plausible explanations.

7. Why doesn't Mr. Beaver trust Edmund when he first meets him? (p. 92)

   FACT: He is able to recognize at first sight Edmund's treachery. (p. 92)

8. How do you know when you can trust someone?

   EVAL: A question of personal experience.

9. Why does Edmund ridicule a stone lion in the Witch's courtyard?

   FACT: It reminds him of Aslan who he thinks has gotten too much praise. (p. 103)

10. When does Edmund conclude that the Queen is evil?

    FACT: When he is forced to go with the Queen on her sledge when she pursues the children and the Beavers. At this time, he also says to himself he can no longer believe that she is good or kind. (p. 124)

11. When with the Witch in her sledge pursuing the children and the Beavers, what happened that for the first time in the story that made Edmund feel sorry for someone besides himself?

     FACT: When Edmund begged the Witch not to turn to stone a Christmas celebration of a group of woodland animals, she gives him a stunning blow in the face. (p. 128)

12. When the children and the Beavers go first meet Aslan what does Lucy ask of him?

     FACT: She asks Aslan if anything can be done to save Edmund. (p. 141)

13. Have you every felt guilty about hurting one of your brothers or sisters?

     EVAL: A question about personal values.

14. Why do all the wood people hate the Witch while "her people" obey her every order?

     INT: A good interpretive question that will evoke differing explanations. (pp. 64, 149, and 165)

15. Why does a lion praise Aslan for his lack of standoffishness?

     FACT: He praises Aslan because he said, "Us Lions. That means him and me!" (p. 191)

THE LION, THE WITCH, AND THE WARDROBE
REVIEW QUIZ ON QUALITIES OF GOOD DISCUSSION QUESTIONS HANDOUT

Directions: On your own paper, mark GOOD if a question would lead to disagreement based on the book. If the question lacks one of the needed qualities, in the margin at the left, mark it:

NC if the question is NOT CLEAR
NS if the question is NOT SPECIFIC and could be asked of any story.
LD for LACKS DOUBT since it cannot be answered in more than one way.
FACT for FACTUAL and cannot be discussed.
EVAL for EVALUATION that could be answered without reading the story.

____ 1. What does Mrs. Beaver mean that there are "two views about humans"? (p. 88)

____ 2. What is the most exciting part of the story?

____ 3. What prophecy are the Beavers talking about?

____ 4. What does the prophecy have to do with the Witch's dwarf and his driving her sledge?

____ 5. Is Peter using Edmund?

____ 6. What's the big deal about Aslan?

____ 7. Why do Peter and Edmund treat each other like they are jerks?

____ 8. What is the role of Mr. Tumnus in the story?

____ 9. Why does Lewis contrast Aslan's leadership with the White Witch's?

____ 10. Have you ever felt like you were living in fantasy world like Narnia?

____ 11. How does the Queen trick Edmund into betraying his brother and sisters?

____ 12. Why do Edmund and Peter fight so much?

____ 13. When does Peter come around to dealing with his problem?

____ 14. Have you ever had a friend that you knew you could depend on whenever you needed help?

____ 15. What does Mr. Beaver mean when he says Aslan "isn't safe but he's good"? (p. 86)

Answer Key

Review Quiz on Qualities of Good Discussion Questions

1. What does Mrs. Beaver mean that there are "two views about humans"? (p. 88)

    GOOD interpretive question for discussion.

2. What is the most exciting part of the story?

    NS: Can be asked of any story.

3. What prophecy are the Beavers talking about?

    FACT: "Down at Cair Paravel there are four thrones and when two Sons of Adam and two Daughters of Eve sit in those four thrones, it will be the end of the Witch's reign as well as her life." (pp. 89, 142)

4. What does the prophecy have to do with the Witch's dwarf and his driving her sledge?

    NC: The question needs explanation. Why do you think there is a connection?

5. Is Peter using Edmund?

    NC: What does "using" mean?

6. What's the big deal about Aslan?

    LD: He is the King of the beasts, son of the Emperor-beyond the Sea, who has returned to Narnia to rid it of the curse of the White Witch.

7. Why do Peter and Edmund treat each other like they are jerks?

    NC: What do you mean by being treated "like a jerk" in this story?

8. What is the role of Mr. Tumnus in the story?

    NS: Can be asked of any character in any story.

9. Why does Lewis contrast Aslan's leadership with the White Witch's?

    GOOD interpretive question for discussion.

10. Have you ever felt like you were living in fantasy world like Narnia?

    EVAL: A question of personal experience.

11. How does the Queen trick Edmund into betraying his brother and sisters?

    FACT: She promises him Turkish Delight and a kingship. (p. 40)

12. Why do Edmund and Peter fight so much?

    NS: What do they fight about? Can you be specific? Do you have a page in mind?

13. When does Peter come around to dealing with his problem?

    NC: What is Peter's "problem"? Can you explain? Do you have a page in mind?

14. Have you ever had a friend that you knew you could depend on whenever you needed help?

    EVAL: A question of personal experience.

15. What does Mr. Beaver mean when he says Aslan "isn't safe but he's good"? (p. 86)

    GOOD interpretive question for discussion

SUGGESTIONS FOR SIX ROLE SHEETS: CAVEAT

The suggestions for these six role sheets are only that, suggestions. They are NOT to be given to the students since that would defeat a major purpose of Literature Circles. According to Principal 6, "Discussion questions [and other ideas in the role sheets] come from the students, not from teachers or textbooks."

Then why offer these ideas at all? So as only to give teachers models of good questions and suggestions that they may sometimes need to come up with when they have a mental block or when they are at a loss for ideas to help their students. In short, these suggestions serve their purpose best when they become a catalyst for a teacher's own ideas and models for their students during mini-lessons before or after discussion.

CHARACTERS CAPTAIN

- ♦ Setting: London, 1941 during World War II and Narnia.
- ♦ Peter Pevensie (William Mosley*): He is the oldest of the four children (18?) who sometimes angers Edmund when he corrects him.
- ♦ Susan Pevensie (Anna Popplewell*): She is the second oldest (17?) who is the voice of reason and common sense.
- ♦ Edmund Pevensie (Skandar Keynes*): Peter's younger brother (16?)—is self-centered, peevish, and entirely resentful of Peter's dominance.
- ♦ Lucy Pevensie (Georgie Henley*): She is the youngest (9) who is very close to her sister, Susan.
- ♦ Digory Kirk (Jim Broadbent*): He is a central character from *The Magician's Nephew* (book 1) who is now an old professor who lives in the country. The Pevensie children have been sent to live with him to escape the air raids in London.
- ♦ Mr. Tumnus (James McAvoy*): a faun who is the first person that Lucy meets in Narnia. From him she learns that all the wood creatures hate the Witch and live in perpetual fear.
- ♦ Mr. and Mrs. Beaver: from these woodland creatures, the four Pevensie first learn about and the prophecy of Narnia: "Down at Cair Paravel there are four thrones and when two Sons of Adam and wo Daughters of Eve sit in those four thrones, it will be the end of the Witch's reign as well as her life." (pp. 89, 142)

♦ White Witch (Tilda Swinton*): The self-appointed Queen of Narnia (Jadis of *The Magician's Nephew*) has cast the country into perpetual winter. Able to turn anyone with her wand into stone, she rules entirely by fear.

♦ Maugrim: A wolf, the Witch's Captain of the Secret Police who suppress entirely any opposition to the rule of Jadis. He arrests Mr. Tumnus for "high treason."

♦ Aslan: Son of the great Emperor-beyond-the- sea, King of the wood and creator of Narnia (*The Magician's Nephew*, book 1) is "on the move." He has returned to Narnia "to set things right"—that is to end the reign of the evil White Witch.

*Actor/actress in the film version.

COLEADERS DISCUSSION QUESTIONS: PREPARED QUESTIONS

1. Why does the author have Aslan overcome the White Witch by sacrificing his own life to save Edmund's?

2. Why does Lewis make the White Witch a nonhuman who is "bad all through"? (p. 88)

3. Why does the narrator tell us that Edmund is not really bad? (p. 96)

4. After his private meeting with Edmund, why does Aslan tell Peter, Susan, and Lucy "there is no need to talk to him about what is past"? (p. 153)

5. Does Aslan accept the Queen's bargain to trade his life for Edmund's because he had no other option? (p. 158)

6. How is Aslan able to overcome death and return to life? (pp. 178-179)

7. After Edmund's near-fatal wound, what does Aslan mean when he asks Lucy, "Must *more* people die for Edmund? (p. 197)

8. Why do we know *but not Edmund* that Aslan exchanged his life for Edmund's? (p. 197)

9. Why does Aslan evoke such different feelings in each of the Pevensie children? (p. 74: Why a feeling of "mysterious horror" in Edmund?)

10. What does Mr. Beaver mean when he says Aslan "isn't safe but he's good"? (p. 86)

11. How can Aslan be "good and terrible at the same time"? (p. 140)

PASSAGE MASTER

Deep Magic: Chapter 15 (pp. 156, 170, 178-179).

WORDSMITH

The average reader will not likely have difficulty with Lewis's vocabulary since his narrator is conscious that his audience is children. However, there are some exotic animals and English references that would have to be defined:

centaur (p. 199)
dungeons (p. 187)
dwarf (p. 32)
faun (chapter 2)

Minotaurs (p. 172)
satyr (p. 125)
Specters (p. 172)
Turkish Delight (p. 40)

CONNECTOR

1. Have you ever been tricked into doing something bad?
2. Have you every felt guilty about hurting one of your brothers or sisters?
3. How do you know when you can trust someone?
4. How can you tell the difference between a true and a phony leader?

MOVIE CRITIC

The Lion, the Witch, and the Wardrobe
http://www.imdb.com/title/tt0363771/
(DVD 135 min.)

1. Introduction: the four Pevensie children.
2. Mrs. Macready
3. The Wardrobe
4. Mr. Tumnus
5. It's Just Your Imagination, Lucy
6. Edmund Meets the Queen
7. Peter, Wake Up!
8. World of Narnia
9. Beavers' Home
10. Queen's Castle
11. They're After Us!
12. Queen's Lair
13. Across the Melting River
14. Aslan's Camp
15. Sir Peter
16. Lion and the Witch

17. Aslan's Sacrifice
19. Battle for Narnia
21. Phoenix
23. Royal Coronation

18. You Have to Lead Us
20. Aslan's Return
22. Peter vs. the Witch

1. Why does the film version have Edmund imprisoned with Mr. Tumnus when he returns to the Witch to betray his brother and sisters? (p. 122)

2. Unlike the original story, why does the film version greatly enlarge Aslan's final battle with the Witch? (Lewis describes this scene in less than two pages (pp. 193-194).

Note: Any English teacher knows that one way to get kids hooked on books and to turn them into life-long readers is to introduce them to an author who has written *a sequence* of stories; for example, a series of related short stories, the Harry Potter adventures, or the seven books of the Chronicles of Narnia. Viewing good film versions of these stories can also increase their enjoyment of good literature. The capsule plot summaries are meant to fill teachers in who may want to offer further suggestions for their students. By the way, the film version of another Narnia story, *Prince Caspian: The Return to Narnia* (book 4) is scheduled for distribution in December 2007.

CHRONICLES OF NARNIA

CAPSULE PLOT SUMMARIES: AN OVERVIEW

Book 1: *The Magician's Nephew*

Digory Kirke's father is a missionary in India and his mother is dying. They live with his Uncle Andrew, an amateur magician, and his aunt. Polly Plummer, the girl next door, and Digory stumble accidentally into Uncle Andrew's study which is off limits. By use of Uncle Andrew's Magic Rings, they journey to the dying world of Charn. In Charn, Digory's curiosity causes him to waken from a charmed sleep the wicked Queen of Charn, Jadis (the White Witch in book 2). When Jadis returns to London with the children and attempts to conquer England, Digory and Polly are determined to return her to Charn. However, they accidentally return her not to Charn but to Narnia at the moment of its creation by Aslan. They also accidentally bring with them Uncle Andrew and his horse Strawberry. The remainder of the story is the account of the children's attempt escape, Jadis, and return to London.

Book 2: *The Lion, the Witch, and the Wardrobe*

Four Pevensie children, Peter, Susan, Edmund, and Lucy have been sent away from London during WW II (because of air raids) to live in the country with Digory Kirke, now an old professor. Lucy discovers in the wardrobe of the mansion an entrance into Narnia. There she meets Mr. Tumnus, a faun, and learns that Narnia is ruled by the White Witch (Jadis) who has cast the country into perpetual winter. The remainder of the story is the continuing conflict between the army of the White Witch and the children who join forces with those Narnians loyal to Aslan. The climax is the death and resurrection of Aslan.

Book 3: *The Horse and His Boy*

This story is set during the reign of Peter, Edmund, Susan and Lucy as described in The *Lion,* and is thus a story within a story. It tells how the boy Shasta of Calormen runs away to avoid being sold as a slave. He is assisted in his escape by Bree, a talking horse of Narnia. They are joined by a girl, Aravis, and her talking horse Hwin, who are also trying to leave Calormen. The remainder of the story is the account of the conflict between Calormen and Narnia and the eventual intervention of Aslan.

Book 4: *Prince Caspian: The Return to Narnia*

This story opens with the same four Pevensie children waiting on a station platform 1 year after their adventure in *The Lion.* They are suddenly drawn into Narnia and find themselves in the ruins of Cair Paravel. Centuries have passed since their previous visit, and learn after rescuing Trumpkin the Dwarf that the Telmarines (Earth-sailors) now rule Narnia. Trumpkin goes on to tell the children that Prince Caspian, who needs their help, was raised by his uncle, Miraz, king of Narnia, and his wife Queen Prunaprismia. From his kindly old tutor, Dr. Cornelius, Prince Caspian learns the previous history of Narnia that King Miraz wants to suppress. The remainder of the story is the account of how Prince Caspian, the true king of Narnia, restores Narnia to its original peace and order with the help of the creatures of "the country of Aslan."

Book 5: *The Voyage of the 'Dawn Treader'*

Book five introduces a new character from England, the unpleasant, snotty Eustace Scrubb, who is receiving a visit from his cousins Edmund and Lucy Pevensie. They are drawn back into Narnia through a picture of a ship, and sail with the former Prince Caspian, now King Caspian X, to search for the seven Narnian lords whom the wicked Miraz sent to explore the unknown Eastern Seas. Reepicheep, the valiant Mouse, hopes that by sailing to the eastern end of the world they will find Aslan's own country. When they finally approach the End of the World, the three children "quiver with happiness" but Reepicheep goes on alone to Aslan's Own Country. The children eventually meet

Aslan and, before he sends them home, he tells them that although Edmund and Lucy will never return to Narnia, they will come to know him better under a different name in their own world. Aslan then declares: "This [that you must learn to know me by another name] was the very reason you were brought to Narnia, that by knowing me here for a little, you may know me better there [in your world]."

Book 6: *The Silver Chair*

A few months after the adventures recounted in *The Voyage of the 'Dawn Treader,'* Eustace and Jill Pole are called away from their horrible coeducational school into Narnia. Seventy Narnian years have passed, and Jill learns form Aslan that King Caspian X is now an old man and that his only son, Prince Rilian, was stolen from him may years before. Commissioned to seek and return the lost prince, Aslan gives Jill four signs by which she and Eustace will be guided in their quest.

Book 7: *The Last Battle*

The last chronicle recounts the end of Narnia 200 years after Aslan was last seen moving visibly through the world. Shift the Ape dresses the simple-minded ass, Puzzle, in the skin of a lion, and so deceives the Talking Beasts and Dwarfs into thinking it is Aslan. By this deception the Calormenes, who worship the false god Tash and who have long wanted to conquer Narnia, are able to overrun the country. When Tirian, the last king of Narnia, is taken captive by the Calormenes, he prays to Aslan for help from those children of this world he has heard about. As a result of his appeal, Eustace and Jill are pulled into Narnia. After a final climatic struggle when Tirian leads the loyal Narnians in the Last Battle against the Calormenes, Aslan holds his Last Judgment. Those found worthy discover that they are in the *real* Narnia of which the other had been "only a shadow or a copy of the real Narnia as our world, England and all, is only a shadow or a copy of something in Aslan's real world." Aslan leads them to the Garden of Paradise, where they are united with Reepicheep and all their friends. They see from that great height all that was worth saving from all worlds joined on to Aslan's Own Country.

ADDENDA: TWO QUESTIONS

ARE THE NARNIA STORIES ALLEGORIES?

Not technically. According to C. S. Lewis "Aslan is an invention giving an imaginary answer to the question, 'What might Christ become like if there really were a world like Narnia and He chose to be incarnate and die and rise again in that world as He actually has done in ours?'" In other words, these stories are more *suppositions* than allegories or extended metaphors which are point-by-point representations of historic events like *Gulliver's Travels* or *Animal Farm*. In short, "I did not say to myself 'Let us represent Jesus as He really is in our world by a Lion in Narnia.' Rather, I said 'Let us *suppose* that there were a land like Narnia and that the Son of God, as He became Man in our world, became a Lion there, and then imagine what would have happened. In short, *what sort of* Incarnation and Passion and Resurrection Christ would have there?"

IS LEWIS'S CHOICE OF A LION FOR ASLAN APPROPRIATE?

In *The New Yorker* (Nov. 22, 2005) Adam Gopnik argues that Aslan is an anti-Christ figure:

> C.S. Lewis' choice of Aslan, the lion, as a Christ symbol was unfortunate. The central point of the Gospel story is that Jesus is not the lion of the faith but the lamb of God, while his other symbolic animal is, specifically, the lowly and bedraggled donkey. The moral force of the Christian story is that the lions are all on the other side. If we had, say, a donkey, a seemingly uninspiring animal from an obscure corner of Narnia, raised as an uncouth and low-caste beast of burden, rallying the mice and rats and weasels and vultures and all the other unclean animals, and then being killed by the lions in as humiliating a manner as possible—a donkey who reemerges, to the shock even of his disciples and devotees, as the king of all creation—now, THAT would be a Christian allegory. A powerful lion, starting life at the top of the food chain, adored by all his subjects and filled with temporal power, killed by a despised evil witch for his power and then reborn to rule, is not the Christian myth."

How would Lewis respond? He would likely invite us to read his story (in *The Last Battle*, book 7) about a donkey that disguises himself as Aslan.

ANIMAL FARM—AN ALLEGORY OF COMMUNISM

Before 1991 the Communist ideology and the Soviet Union were a major threat to the Western democracies. In *Animal Farm* Orwell demonstrated the moral bankruptcy of the Russian Communist system.

An allegory is an artistic device in which the characters and events of the story represent something else. The literal content of an allegorical work is less important than its symbolic meaning. Allegory is employed in literature, visual arts, drama, and ballet. *Animal Farm* is one of the premier works of modern fiction that uses allegory.

Communism is an economic/political system in which all of the factories, farms, real estate, and other means of economic production are owned and controlled by the community for the benefit of all. Each person is supposed to work according to his ability and to receive benefits from society according to his needs. Theoretically, in the ultimate stages of the development of society, when all the attributes of capitalism have been abolished, government would become unnecessary. In reality communism has been associated with repressive dictatorial regimes which did not release the energies of the people sufficiently to attain a high standard of living.

Communist social philosophy was developed by Karl Marx and Friedrich Engels in the nineteenth century. It became a potent worldwide force in 1917 when adherents to its theories, the Bolsheviks, took power in Russia and created the Soviet Union. Since the collapse of the Soviet Union in 1991, Communism has been abandoned by most governments and is no longer considered a threat to the Western democracies.

The two other major theories of how economies are to be managed are capitalism and socialism. Capitalism is a system in which the means of production and distribution are privately owned and are managed for profit. The exchange of goods and services takes place through a free market system governed by supply and demand. The United States and most countries in the world have modified capitalism by imposing government regulation on the production of goods and services and on the markets when necessary to ensure the public welfare. Examples of these regulations are the wage and hour laws, health and safety codes, antitrust laws, and product liability law suits.

Socialism is an economic system in which the most important means of production, as well as the means of distribution of goods and services, are owned by the state and managed for the welfare of society as a whole. In a socialist state, for example, the natural resources, factories, large farms, the banking system, and the markets would be owned and operated by the state. Socialism, like communism, was a reaction to the vast inequalities of wealth suffered by capitalist Europe in the eighteenth and nineteenth centuries. There have been many governments in Europe and the Third World with socialist goals which they were not able to fully attain. Some aspects of the socialist system have been, to varying degrees, adopted in Europe and the United States to ameliorate the excesses of capitalism. These include, welfare (income assistance for the destitute), national retirement plans (Social Security), medical care (limited to the poor and the elderly in the U.S.) and unemployment insurance, the U.S. Postal Service, the Tennessee Valley Authority, municipal electric power companies, and state stores that sell liquor.

The consensus in the United States and most of the Western World is that the most efficient form of economic organization is a modified capitalism in which most of the means of production and distribution are privately owned but are also subject to government regulation to keep markets free, prevent abuses and ensure public safety. A safety net is provided to redistribute wealth to those unable to provide for themselves, such as the poor, the handicapped and the elderly.

One of the saving graces of humanity is the ability to find humor in terrible circumstances: The citizens of the Soviet Union created a large number of jokes about their repressive government. For example:

♦ What is the difference between capitalism and Soviet socialism? *Answer:* Capitalism is based on the exploitation of man by man. Under Soviet socialism it is the opposite.

♦ A new prisoner arrives at a prison camp and is asked by another prisoner about the length of this sentence. "Seven years," he replies, "but there was no crime. I didn't do anything." The other prisoner responds, "You must be lying, the sentence for nothing is only five years."

Source: http://www.teachwithmovies.com/CMP/guides/animal-farm.html

IS ASLAN A CHRIST FIGURE?

Victor Moeller

Yes and no. On one hand, C. S. Lewis certainly thinks he is: Aslan is "an invention giving an imaginary answer to the question, 'What might Christ become like, if there really were a world like Narnia and He chose to be incarnate and die and rise again in *that* world as he actually has done in ours?'" (*Letters of C. S. Lewis.* 1988, p. 475). Nevertheless, Lewis denies that the *Chronicles of Narnia* were allegories—point-for-point correspondences between our world an another: "I am not writing another *Pilgrim's Progress* [or an *Animal Farm*]. I did not say to myself 'Let us represent Jesus as He really is in our world by a Lion in Narnia.' ... I said 'Let us *suppose that* there were a land like Narnia *and that* there were a land like Narnia *and that* the Son of God, as He became a Man in our world, became a Lion there, *and then* imagine what would happen." In short, *what sort of* Incarnation and Passion and Resurrection Christ would have there?" (p. 476).

Some critics, Ryken and Mead, agree: "Literary lineages for God as a lion are readily established. To the Western imagination from time immemorial, the lion has been 'king of beasts,' a figure of authority. The name Aslan is the Turkish word for lion. Lewis's friend Charles Williams has written a novel entitled, *The Place of the Lion.* In the Bible, Christ is 'the Lion of the tribe of Judah' (Revelation 5:5). As for the statement in chapter 8 (of the LWW, p. 79), 'Wrong will be right, when Aslan comes in sight, the sound of his roar' it is reminiscent of the

OT prophecy of Amos (3:8): 'The lion roared; who will not fear?'" (*A Reader's Guide Through the Wardrobe*. 2005, pp. 65-66).

On the other hand, others disagree. In *The New Yorker* (Nov. 22, 2005) Adam Gopnik argues portraying Aslan as a Christ figure is a mistake: "C. S. Lewis' choice of Aslan, the lion, as a Christ symbol was unfortunate. The central point of the Gospel story is that Jesus is not the lion of the faith but the lamb of God, while his other symbolic animal is, specifically, the lowly and bedraggled donkey. The moral force of the Christian story is that the lions are all on the other side. If we had, say, a donkey, a seemingly uninspiring animal from an obscure corner of Narnia, raised as an uncouth and low-caste beast of burden, rallying the mice and rats and weasels and vultures and all the other unclean animals, and then being killed by the lions in as humiliating a manner as possible—a donkey who reemerges, to the shock even of his disciples and devotees, as the king of all creation—now, *that* would be a Christian allegory. A powerful lion, starting life at the top of the food chain, adored by all his subjects and filled with temporal power, killed by a despised evil witch for his power and then reborn to rule, is not the Christian myth."

With whom do I agree? The question needs revision. We should be asking two questions: (1) Is Lewis' choice of a lion for Aslan appropriate? and (2) In Narnia, is Aslan portrayed as an action hero more than a Christ figure? For Adam Gopnik, the answer to the first question is clearly no because Aslan is so inconsistent with the Lamb of God and the Good Shepherd—the first metaphors of Jesus in the primitive church. Like Gopnik, I am also not convinced by the argument of Ryken and Mead who offer meager references to the Old Testament and a single reference in the New Testament from Revelation which, in context extols the Lamb of God, not the lion. In reply to the second question, does the resurrection scene in the film make the same mistake that Mel Gibson does in his *Passion of Christ*? While Gibson gives Jesus all of 85 seconds to the resuscitation on Easter to leave the tomb and begin anew His battle with the world that rejects him, Lewis's measured description of Easter morning has Christ's Deeper Magic conquer Death (LWW, pp. 176-182.)

And what are we to make of the interpretation of the film version's climatic confrontation between Aslan and the White Witch? Lewis describes this showdown in only three sentences of 59 words (LWW, p. 194) while the movie dwells on it with special effects for 20 minutes. Here again, as in Gibson's movie, Aslan becomes an the action hero who takes charge. There's no Deeper Magic here.

Where would Lewis be in this debate today? How would he respond? I am reasonably confident to point out that he would say three things:

♦ My resurrection scene is true to the Gospels which are all in remarkable accord on this foundational belief of the first Christians in the resurrected Christ.

- Unlike the movie, in my book Aslan's final battle with the White Witch is subordinated to His victory over Death in His Resurrection.
- Finally, I invite skeptics like Adam Gopnik to read my last story, *The Last Battle*, where a donkey disguised in lion skins becomes Aslan, an anti-Christ who momentarily deceives his followers.

8

IS TECHNOLOGY AS MUCH A BLESSING AS A CURSE?

As is so often characteristic of Ray Bradbury's science fiction, "The Veldt," concerns itself with the benefits and dehumanizing dangers of modern technology. "It [the nursery] had cost half again as much as their Happy Life Home, but nothing is too good for your children," according to George Hadley. Unlike her husband, who had nothing but admiration for the technical genius who had conceived the nursery, Lydia feared that it was "out of control." Their two emotionally disturbed children, 10-year-old Peter and his sister, Wendy, "lived for the nursery" which caught the telepathic emanations of their minds and created life to fill their every desire. Whatever they thought appeared on the four-walled television room that entirely engulfed them and became their virtual environment. This unique room was supposed to help the children work off their neuroses in a healthful way. However, their thoughts were not about *Green Mansions* and Rima but always about a veldtland filled with roaring lions feasting on zebras and baby giraffes. In short, the children were obsessed with violence in the wild and thoughts of death. And even after the Hadleys realize the nursery has become a kind of surrogate parent, they are unable to do anything about it—even after seeking the help of a child psychologist, David McClean. The basic question is then, "Why does Bradbury have the Hadleys discover too late that something is wrong with their family life?" Why do the children kill their parents after wanting them to turn off their nursery? At what point does Bradbury suggest that technology can threaten and even destroy family relationships? And, in "The Veldt," why does Bradbury imply that imaginary lions killed real people (George and Lydia)?

How much is the "Happy Life Home" of Bradbury's story like "What our homes will look like in 2107." Suggestion: before having your students read and discuss this nonfiction followup reading, have them draw up a list of the ways that future technology will affect our lives at home.

While Bradbury's vision of the future of technology is always skeptical and cautionary and even alarming, Isaac Asimov is nearly always optimistic and eager to extol its virtues. In his sequence of related stories on the history of robotics, *Robbie*, the narrator, Susan Calvin who joined U.S. Robots and Mechanical Men in 2008, traces the development of robots from rather crude machines through increasing sophistication until they become virtually indistinguishable from humans in 2050. The first story, "Robbie," takes place before Susan Calvin joined U.S. Robots in 1998. She is present in the story as a teenage girl who observes people asking questions of the first talking robot that has been put on public display. Robbie is a nursemaid for 8-year old Gloria Weston who can do all the things a human companion could do, except talk, and, he has much greater patience. As in "The Veldt," the parents, George and Grace Weston, disagree about Robbie's place in their daughter's development. George regards Gloria's companion as "the best darn robot money can buy" even if it cost him a half year's income. Grace, on the other hand, is so worried about "that terrible machine," she wants to get rid of it. She knows it cannot be healthy that Gloria prefers to play with Robbie, rather than other children. During his 2 years with Gloria, Robbie does not leave his charge for a moment. But Grace Weston also fears that something "might go wrong" with Robbie. After all, he is a machine and machines can and do sometimes fail. Our basic question then becomes: With whose attitude toward Robbie does Asimov want us to agree—with George's or with Grace's? Ample evidence in the story makes this a legitimate issue.

Although, the 2004 movie version of Asimov's collection of short stories, "I, Robot," was a commercial success, it failed to impress Asimov loyalists. While some critics defend it as a story in its own right, others point out that the screenplay, by Jeff Vintar and Akiva Goldsman, has but one explicit connection with Asimov's original story—the Three Laws of Robotics: (1) A robot may not injure a human being or, through inaction, allow a human being to come to harm. (2) A robot must obey orders given it by human beings except where such orders would conflict with the First Law. (3) A robot must protect its own existence as long as such protection does not conflict with the First or Second Law. The Three Laws become the organizing principle and unifying theme for Asimov's *Foundation Trilogy*. The movie's chief departure from Asimov (whose stories are almost devoid of violence) is its action scenes involving police and crowds fighting or evading mobs of rampaging robots. "Robot as menace," is precisely the kind of story that Asimov abhorred. In contrast, Asimov's robot stories were the first to treat robots as useful creations that could have positive interactions with humans.

To decide for yourself if you think the movie is worth your students' time and discussion, check out the Wikipedia free encyclopedia article at: http://en.wikipedia.org/wiki/I,_Robot_(movie)

Although Asimov's focus is on the history of robotics in the stories of *I, Robot*, they all assume that space travel has become common place and available to virtually everyone—regardless of social or financial status. But what about the dawn of the space age when Sputnik joined "the sublime company of the heavenly bodies" in our solar system 50 years ago? On October 4, 1957 two contemporary authors, Hannah Arendt a German-American political theorist, and an anonymous spokesman for the Smithsonian reported this historic event in remarkable contrast. Arendt is euphoric while the Smithsonian is cynical. With the advent of the millennium, James Glieck was asked to reassess the historic significance of Sputnik. These "Three Viewpoints on Sputnik" will give your students a rare opportunity to understand and to explain the reasons for such differing estimations. Suggestion: before discussion, have your students make notes on each of the three articles that answer three questions: (1) How does the tone of each passage differ? (2) Why does the tone of each passage differ? and (3) What is each writer's purpose?

"The Veldt"

Lesson Plan 14

1. Focus: Would you like to live in a house that could serve your meals, warm your bed, remind you of things you had to do today, had mental-telepathy television, and cleaned itself? (Journal or Response Log)

2. Objective:
    ♦ To understand the nature and requirements of six role sheets on this short story that participants will share in their small-group discussions.
    ♦ To review the Three Kinds of Questions and Qualities of Good Discussion Questions.

3. Purpose: To prepare students for small-group discussion.

4. Input and Modeling: Plot-Check Quiz on Three Kinds of Questions and Exercise on the Qualities of Good Questions on the short story by Ray Bradbury.

5. Checking for Understanding: Review the Plot-Check Quiz and the Exercise on Qualities of Good Questions.

6. Guided Practice: Review the content of each of the six role sheets: Discussion Coleaders, Characters Captain, Passage Master, and Connector.

7. Closure: Extol good examples and make suggestions for those that need improvement.

Sources: Bradbury, R. (1965). The veldt. In *The vintage Bradbury* (pp. 13-28). New York: Random House; The veldt. In *The illustrated man* (pp. 7-19). New York: Doubleday.

Internet: American Short Story Project: Ray Bradbury blog on "The Veldt" http://caxton.stockton.edu/shortstoryreb/

"THE VELDT":
PLOT-CHECK QUIZ
HANDOUT

Directions: On your own paper, answer each question briefly in the space beneath it and then identify the type of each question: print FACT for factual, INT for interpretation, and EVAL for evaluation.

_____ 1. Why do the children kill their parents?

_____ 2. Why is David McClean brought in to look at the nursery?

_____ 3. Even after the Hadleys realize that the nursery is a real danger, why are they unable to do anything to improve their family life?

_____ 4. Would you like to live in a house like the Hadley's?

_____ 5. What personal belonging did George find in the nursery?

_____ 6. Why do George and Lydia want to take a family vacation?

_____ 7. Why does Lydia tell George "it can't hurt" to turn on the nursery just one more time?

_____ 8. Can too many gadgets and creature comforts weaken family relationships?

_____ 9. After the death of their parents, why does Bradbury have the children invite Mr. McClean to share their picnic lunch?

_____ 10. How would Bradbury have us explain how imaginary lions could kill real people?

_____ 11. What was Peter and Wendy's favorite scene in the nursery?

_____ 12. What personal belonging does Lydia find in the nursery?

_____ 13. Why does the children's preference for the nursery so worry their parents?

_____ 14. Why do George and Lydia finally realize that the screams in the nursery were so familiar?

_____ 15. Have your parents ever denied you something that you wanted more than anything in the world?

Answer Key

Plot-Check Quiz

1. Why do the children kill their parents?

   INT: Several correct answers are possible depending on the story.

2. Why is David McClean brought in to look at the nursery?

   FACT: It was out of control. (p. 23)

3. Even after the Hadleys realize that the nursery is a real danger, why are they unable to do anything to improve their family life?

   INT: Several correct answers are possible depending on the story.

4. Would you like to live in a house like the Hadley's?

   EVAL: A question about personal experience.

5. What personal belonging did George find in the nursery?

   FACT: His wallet. (p. 20)

6. Why do George and Lydia want to take a family vacation?

   FACT: They thought their 10-year-old children needed a vacation from fantasy and needed more to do. (pp. 16, 18)

7. Why does Lydia tell George "it can't hurt" to turn on the nursery just one more time?

   INT: Several correct answers are possible depending on the story.

8. Can too many gadgets and creature comforts weaken family relationships?

   EVAL: A question about personal values.

9. After the death of their parents, why does Bradbury have the children invite Mr. McClean to share their picnic lunch?

   INT: Several correct answers are possible depending on the story.

10. How would Bradbury have us explain how imaginary lions could kill real people?

    INT: Several correct answers are possible depending on the story.

11. What was Peter and Wendy's favorite scene in the nursery?

    FACT: An African veldt with lions eating their prey. (p. 22)

12. What personal belonging does Lydia find in the nursery?

   FACT: Her scarf. (p. 25)

13. Why does the children's preference for the nursery so worry their parents?

   INT: Several correct answers are possible depending on the story.

14. Why do George and Lydia finally realize that the screams in the nursery were so familiar?

   FACT: The screams were their own. (pp. 22, 28)

15. Have your parents ever denied you something that you wanted more than anything in the world?

   EVAL: A question of personal experience.

"The Veldt"

Review Quiz on Qualities of Good Discussion Questions Handout

Directions: On your own paper, mark GOOD if a question would lead to a disagreement based on the story. If the question lacks one of the needed qualities, mark it:

NC if the question is NOT CLEAR and would have to be explained.
NS if the question is NOT SPECIFIC and could be asked of any story.
LD for LACKS DOUBT since it cannot be answered in more than one way.
FACT for FACTUAL and cannot be discussed.

_____ 1. What kind of relationship is there between the children and their parents?

_____ 2. Why do the parents just let their children go like that?

_____ 3. Were the children only dreaming about lions in a veldt?

_____ 4. Why is the nursery more important to the children than their parents?

_____ 5. What is the role of Mr. McClean in the story?

_____ 6. Is technology as much a blessing as a curse?

_____ 7. Why is the title of the story "The Veldt"?

_____ 8. Why don't they tell their kids the truth?

_____ 9. Why do the children go into hysterics?

_____ 10. What is the point of the story?

_____ 11. Why do the children kill their parents?

_____ 12. Why does Peter act like a jerk?

_____ 13. Do the parents really care about their children's welfare?

_____ 14. Why are the children so calm after killing their parents?

_____ 15. Why do the Hadleys ask a psychologist to examine the nursery when they know that it is mechanical and could be turned off with a switch?

ANSWER KEY

REVIEW QUIZ ON QUALITIES OF GOOD DISCUSSIONS QUESTIONS

1. What kind of relationship is there between the children and their parents?

    NS: Can be asked of any characters in any story.

2. Why do the parents just let their children go like that?

    NC: What does "go on like that" mean?

3. Were the children only dreaming about lions in a veldt?

    LD: Since there is no evidence of dreaming, the answer has to be no.

4. Why is the nursery more important to the children than their parents?

    GOOD interpretive question for discussion.

5. What is the role of Mr. McClean in the story?

    NS: Can be asked of any character in any story.

    FACT: He is a psychologist who Mr. Hadley has asked for advice. (p. 24)

6. Is technology as much a blessing as a curse?

    EVAL: A question about personal values.

7. Why is the title of the story "The Veldt"?

    NS: Can be asked about the title of any story.

8. Why don't they tell their kids the truth?

    NC: Does "they" mean the parents? If so, "what truth"?

9. Why do the children go into hysterics?

    FACT: Their parents plan to shut down the nursery. (p. 26)

10. What is the point of the story?

    NS: If "point" means theme or message, the question can be asked of any story.

11. Why do the children kill their parents?

    GOOD interpretive question for discussion.

12. Why does Peter act like a jerk?

    NC: How is Peter a "jerk"? When?

13. Do the parents really care about their children's good?

    LD: Yes. There is no evidence that would make us think that they don't.

14. Why are the children so calm after killing their parents?

    GOOD interpretive question for discussion.

15. Why do the Hadleys ask a psychologist to examine the nursery when they know that it is mechanical and could be turned off with a switch?

    GOOD interpretive question for discussion.

SUGGESTIONS FOR SIX ROLE SHEETS: CAVEAT

The suggestions for these six role sheets are only that, suggestions. They are NOT to be given to the students since that would defeat a major purpose of Literature Circles. According to Principal 6, "Discussion questions [and other ideas in the role sheets] come from the students, not from teachers or textbooks."

Then why offer these ideas at all? So as only to give teachers models of good questions and suggestions that they may sometimes need to come up with when they have a mental block or when they are at a loss for ideas to help their students. In short, these suggestions serve their purpose best when they become a catalyst for a teacher's own ideas and models for their students during mini-lessons before or after discussion.

COLEADER DISCUSSION QUESTIONS: PREPARED QUESTIONS

1. Even after the Hadleys realize that the nursery is a real danger, why are they unable to do anything to improve their family life? (pp. 16, 22)

2. Why do the Hadley's see the nursery as harmful to their children but not to themselves? (pp. 16-17)

3. Why does the nursery fail to respond to George's change from a veldt into Aladdin and his lamp? (p. 19)

4. When the Hadleys believe that their children have broken into the nursery, why do they go back to sleep? (p. 22)

5. Why don't the Hadley's take David McClean's advice to have the nursery torn down and their children brought to him for treatment? (p. 24)

6. Why do the Hadley's continue to give into to their children even after they realize how spoiled they have become? (pp. 24-26)

7. Why does the author have the children kill their parents? (pp. 27-28)

8. Why are Peter and Wendy so calm after killing their parents? (p. 28)

9. Why is the nursery more important to the children than their parents? (p. 24)

10. Why do the children create death scenes in the nursery? (p. 17)

11. Does Bradbury want us to agree with George's belief that the children are too young (10) to know what death is? (p. 17)

12. Why does Bradbury want us to know that before the children had become obsessed with the veldt, they had used the nursery for scenes from famous children's books? (p. 18)

13. Why do the children put their father's wallet and their mother's scarf in the nursery? (pp. 20 and 25)

14. Why doesn't Bradbury give Mr. McClean a chance to rid the children of their "death thoughts"?

15. Why do George, Lydia, and Peter all refer to the house as if it had a will of its own? (pp. 18, 24, 25, 27)

16. Does Bradbury want us to feel sorry for George and Lydia for being unable to help their children have normal lives?

17. Why does the author end the story with Peter and Wendy asking Mr. McClean to share their lunch with them? p. 28

Characters Captain

♦ Setting: Sometime in the distant future, 2020?

♦ George Hadley: Although the father of Peter and Wendy marvels at the mechanical genius who had conceived their Happy Life Home, he is worried that their children have become obsessed with one room, the nursery.

♦ Lydia Hadley: George's wife is more concerned than he about their children's mental health. Indeed, she believes that the nursery has become a surrogate parent.

◆ Peter Hadley: The 10-year-old son who tells his father that he hates him when he realizes that he plans to shut down the nursery.

◆ Wendy Hadley: The 10-year old sister of Peter who is also obsessed with the nursery.

◆ Mr. McClean: George turns to David McClean, a psychologist, for analysis of the nursery and advice about how he can help his children who are as out of control as the nursery seems to be.

WORDSMITH

abruptly (p. 15)

abstractedly (p. 19)

appalled (p. 15)

conjuring (p. 17)

emanations (p. 18)

insufferable (p. 21)

neuroses (p. 21)

odorphonics (p. 14)

paranoia (p. 23)

psychologist (p. 13)

relish (p. 23)

Rima (in Green Mansions) (p. 20)

superreactionary (p. 21)

sonics (p. 22)

telepathic (p. 18)

veldt (p. 14)

PASSAGE MASTER

After George tells the children that he plans to shut down the house, "The two children were in hysterics" (pp. 26-28) and the resolution. My students respond to this passage when they hear it as Reader's Theater—when parts have been assigned and read as a dialogue between George, Lydia, Peter, and the narrator. As a follow up, I always have the students discuss or write a journal on: Who gave the most dramatic and convincing performance. In other words, which character's emotional expression was more convincing.

CONNECTOR

The Connector's contribution to discussion is to write and raise at least four evaluation questions—two about personal experience and two about personal values. Suggestions:

1. Have you ever felt pampered to the point of boredom? (experience)

2. Would you want to like in a house like the Hadley's Happy Life Home? If so, why? If not, what problems could you predict? (experience)

3. Why can technological advances never fill all our human needs? (values)

4. Is technology as much a blessing as a curse? (values)

"Robbie"

Lesson Plan 15

1. Focus:

Would you like to have a humanoid robot at your beck and call? (Journal or Response Log)

2. Objective:

♦ To understand the nature and requirements of six role sheets on this novel that participants will share in their small-group discussions.

♦ To review the Three Kinds of Questions and Qualities of Good Discussion Questions.

3. Purpose:

To prepare students for small-group discussion.

4. Input and Modeling:

Plot-Check Quiz on Three Kinds of Questions and Exercise on the Qualities of Good Questions on the short story by Isaac Asimov.

5. Checking for Understanding:

Review the Plot-Check Quiz and the Exercise on Qualities of Good Questions.

6. Guided Practice:

Review the content of each of the six role sheets: Discussion Coleaders, Characters Captain, Passage Master, Connector, and Movie Critic.

7. Closure:

Extol good examples and make suggestions for those that need improvement.

Source: Asimov, I. (1977). Robbie. In *I robot* (pp. 11-30). New York: Ballatine Books.

Film: Wikipedia: http://en.wikipedia.org/wiki/I,_Robot_(movie)

Internet: Templeton Gate: Introduction to *I Robot* and "Robbie"
    http://templetongate.tripod.com/irobot.htm

"ROBBIE"

PLOT-CHECK QUIZ
HANDOUT

Directions: On your own paper, answer each question briefly in the space beneath it and then identify the type of each question: print FACT for factual, INT for interpretation, and EVAL for evaluation.

_____ 1. Unlike George, why does Grace Weston fear Robbie?

_____ 2. Why does Asimov give Robbie human emotions and yet remind us that it is still a robot?

_____ 3. Are people today overdependent on machines?

_____ 4. Why does Gloria think her parents are taking her to New York City?

_____ 5. How does Grace Weston plan to make Gloria forget Robbie? (p. 20)

_____ 6. Why is Gloria portrayed as a spoiled child?

_____ 7. How does George Weston plan to make Gloria forget Robbie?

_____ 8. Had you been Gloria's mother or father, would you have allowed her to keep Robbie?

_____ 9. Unlike Grace, why is George unable to see any harm or danger in Gloria's relationship with Robbie?

_____ 10. Why does Gloria fiercely insist that Robbie is not a machine?

_____ 11. Does Gloria think "Cinderella" is a story for babies?

_____ 12. Do most of the neighbors agree with Grace Weston that Robbie is dangerous?

_____ 13. Why does Gloria think she knows why her parents take her to New York City?

_____ 14. Why does Asimov have George interrupt Mr. Struthers when he is explaining the future advantages of robots in daily life?

_____ 15. While visiting the robot factory in New York, why were the human supervisors unable to save Gloria from being crushed by the tractor?

NOTE: Which of these factual questions be revised as interpretive questions?

ANSWER KEY

PLOT-CHECK QUIZ

1. Unlike George, why does Grace Weston fear Robbie?

    FACT: It is a machine that may go berserk and harm Gloria. (p. 17)

2. Why does Asimov give Robbie human emotions and yet remind us that it is still a robot?

    INT: More than one correct answer is possible depending on evidence in the story. (pp. 14-17, and 29)

3. Are people today overdependent on machines?

    EVAL: A question about personal values and experience.

4. Why does Gloria think her parents are taking her to New York City?

    FACT: She thinks that detectives will find Robbie for her. (p. 22)

5. How does Grace Weston plan to make Gloria forget Robbie? (p. 20)

    FACT: She hopes to replace it with a dog and change her environment.

6. Why is Gloria portrayed as a spoiled child?

    INT: More than one correct answer is possible depending on evidence in the story. (pp. 13, 20, and 26)

7. How does George Weston plan to make Gloria forget Robbie?

    FACT: He will have her find Robbie working in a robot factory to realize that it is only a machine. (p. 26)

8. Had you been Gloria's mother or father, would you have allowed her to keep Robbie?

    EVAL: A question about personal values.

9. Unlike Grace, why is George unable to see any harm or danger in Gloria's relationship with Robbie?

    INT: More than one correct answer is possible depending on evidence in the story. (pp. 17-18, and 29)

10. Why does Gloria fiercely insist that Robbie is not a machine?

    INT: More than one correct answer is possible depending on evidence in the story. (p. 20)

11. Does Gloria think "Cinderella" is a story for babies?

    FACT: Yes. That is what she tells Robbie. (p. 14)

12. Do most of the neighbors agree with Grace Weston that Robbie is dangerous?

    FACT: Yes. (p. 17)

13. Why does Gloria think she knows why her parents take her to New York City?

    INT: More than one correct answer is possible depending on evidence in the story. (p. 22)

14. Why does Asimov have George interrupt Mr. Struthers when he is explaining the future advantages of robots in daily life?

    INT: more than one correct answer is possible depending on evidence in the story. p. 27

15. While visiting the robot factory in New York, why were the human supervisors unable to save Gloria from being crushed by the tractor?

    FACT: They failed because they were "only human." p. 28

"Robbie"

Review Quiz on Qualities of Good Discussion Questions Handout

Directions: On your own paper, mark GOOD if a question would lead to a disagreement based on the story. If the question lacks one of the needed qualities, mark it:

NC if the question is NOT CLEAR and would have to be explained.
NS if the question is NOT SPECIFIC and could be asked of any story.
LD for LACKS DOUBT since it cannot be answered in more than one way.
FACT for FACTUAL and cannot be discussed.
EVAL for EVALUATION and not about understanding the story.

_____ 1.   What kind of relationship does Gloria have with her parents?

_____ 2.   What's wrong with Robbie?

_____ 3.   Do Mr. and Mrs. Weston really disagree about robots?

_____ 4.   What is the biggest reason for George and Grace's disagreement about Robbie's role in their daughter's life?

_____ 5.   Does George have more trust than Grace in the reliability of robots?

_____ 6.   How important are robots in our lives today?

_____ 7.   Why is Mrs. Weston so stupid about robots?

_____ 8.   What is the point of the story?

_____ 9.   Why does Gloria go willingly with her parents to New York?

_____ 10. What is the role of Mr. Struthers in the story?

_____ 11. Why does Asimov begin the story with Gloria playing with Robbie?

_____ 12. Why does Gloria keep putting on the way she does?

_____ 13. Does Gloria really think that Robbie is not a machine?

_____ 14. With whose attitude towards Robbie does Asimov want us to agree—George or Grace Weston's?

ANSWER KEY

REVIEW QUIZ ON QUALITIES OF GOOD DISCUSSION QUESTIONS

1. What kind of relationship does Gloria have with her parents?

   NS: Can be asked of the relationships of any character(s) in any story.

2. What's wrong with Robbie?

   NC: What does "wrong" mean? It needs explanation.

3. Do Mr. and Mrs. Weston really disagree about robots?

   LD: Yes they do in several ways. See question 4 for an improvement.

4. What is the biggest reason for George and Grace's disagreement about Robbie's role in their daughter's life?

   GOOD interpretive question for discussion. (pp. 14-16 and 20)

5. Does George have more trust than Grace in the reliability of robots?

   LD: The answer is yes because no evidence supports the contrary.

6. How important are robots in our lives today?

   EVAL: The question asks for an answer that is outside the story.

7. Why is Mrs. Weston so stupid about robots?

   NC: How is she stupid about robots? "Stupid" needs explanation

8. What is the point of the story?

   NS: If "point" means message or theme, it can be asked of any story.

9. Why does Gloria go willingly with her parents to New York?

   FACT: She thinks that they are going there to find Robbie.

10. What is the role of Mr. Struthers in the story?

    NS: Can be asked of any character in any story. What do you want to know about his role in "Robbie"? Can you be more specific?

11. Why does Asimov begin the story with Gloria playing with Robbie?

    GOOD interpretive question for discussion.

12. Why does Gloria keep putting on the way she does?

   NC: What does "putting on the way she does" mean? Explanation needed.

13. Does Gloria really think that Robbie is not a machine?

   LD: Yes. She's says he's "a person just like you and me and he is my friend." (p. 20) No evidence would make us doubt her meaning.

14. With whose attitude toward Robbie does Asimov want us to agree—George or Grace Weston's?

   GOOD interpretive question for discussion.

SUGGESTIONS FOR SIX ROLE SHEETS:
CAVEAT

The suggestions for these six role sheets are only that, suggestions. They are NOT to be given to the students since that would defeat a major purpose of Literature Circles. According to Principal 6, "Discussion questions [and other ideas in the role sheets] come from the students, not from teachers or textbooks."

Then why offer these ideas at all? So as only to give teachers models of good questions and suggestions that they may sometimes need to come up with when they have a mental block or when they are at a loss for ideas to help their students. In short, these suggestions serve their purpose best when they become a catalyst for a teacher's own ideas and models for their students during mini-lessons before or after discussion.

COLEADER DISCUSSION QUESTIONS:
PREPARED QUESTIONS

1. Why does Asimov have George Weston (p. 17) regard Robbie as a great benefit while Grace Weston (p. 16) see it as a threat and potential danger?
2. Why does Asimov give Robbie human emotions? (pp. 14, 15, and 29)
3. Why does George place more trust in Robbie than in a human nurse-maid? (p. 16)
4. Why does Gloria reject a more sophisticated robot for Robbie? (pp. 25-26)
5. Why does Susan Calvin regard robots as a better "breed" than humans? (Introduction)
6. Why does Grace say Robbie has no "soul" when she knows it is a robot? (p. 16)
7. Why is Grace so concerned about her neighbors' opinion of Robbie? (p. 16)
8. Why does Grace think that "something might go wrong" with Robbie when it has never done anything to endanger Gloria? (p. 16)
9. Why does Asimov have Gloria insist that Robbie is not a machine? (p. 20)
10. Does Asimov want us to agree with Grace that Gloria could be harmed psychologically and emotionally by overdependence on Robbie? (pp. 20-21)

11. Why is Gloria unimpressed with the much-publicized Talking Robot that she met in New York City? (pp. 24-26)

12. Why does Asimov end the story by having Robbie save Gloria's life? (pp. 28-29)

13. Why does George Weston admit that he had arranged for Gloria to "find" Robbie working in a factory? (p. 28)

14. Why does Grace Weston agree to let Robbie return to Gloria after he saves her life. (p. 29)

15. With whose attitude toward Robbie does Asimov want us to agree—George or Grace Weston's?

CHARACTERS CAPTAIN

♦ Setting: A village in upstate New York and New York City. "Robbie" was written in 1940 as the first story of nine stories on the history of robotics in *I, Robot*. The story takes place in 1998.

♦ Susan Calvin: She is being interviewed after working for U.S. Robot and Mechanical Men or 50 years.

♦ Robbie: A nonvocal nursemaid robot that was made in 1996. His job was to take care of Gloria Weston.

♦ Gloria Weston: An 8-year-old girl for whom Robbie has become her best friend and playmate.

♦ Grace Weston: Gloria's anxious mother who is entirely worried that Robbie may some day "go berserk and harm Gloria."

♦ George Weston: In contrast to her mother, George is confident that Robbie has been properly programed "for only one purpose really—to be the companion of a little child.... He's a machine—made so. That's more than I can say for humans."

♦ The Talking Robot: The First Talking Robot on display in the Museum of Science and Industry in New York City is "*a tour de force*, a thoroughly impractical device, possessing publicity value only." (p. 24)

♦ Mr. Struthers: General Manager of U.S. Robot and Mechanical Men Inc., gives tour of the factory to the Weston family.

WORDSMITH

parallelepiped (p. 12)
ponderously, irrefutable (p. 13)
quavered, disconsolate (p. 15)

visivox (p. 18)
morosely (p. 19)
retorted, tartly (p. 22)
peremptorily, stratosphere (p. 23)
tour de force (p. 24)
erratic, incoherent (p. 25)
query (p. 26)
incredulous (p. 27)
formidable (p. 28)
abstractedly (p. 29)

PASSAGE MASTER

Early in the story, after the narrator describes Gloria playing with Robbie, the next scene introduces the serious conflict between her parents, George and Grace Weston, that begins with "George Weston was comfortable" (p. 15 bottom) and continues on all of page 16 and two thirds of page 17 ending with "And with that he walked out of the room in a huff." My students respond to this passage when they hear it as Reader's Theater—when parts have been assigned and read as a dialogue between George and Grace and the narrator's observations. As a follow up, I always have the students discuss or write a journal on: (1) Do you agree with the way that Asimov resolves the conflict between Gloria's parents and the role of Robbie in her life? and/or (2) Who gave the most dramatic and convincing performance. In other words, which character's emotional expression was more convincing.

CONNECTOR

The Connector's contribution to discussion is to write and raise at least four evaluation questions—two about personal experience and two about personal values. Suggestions:

1. Have you ever seen an "artificial intelligence" machine? (experience)
2. Have you ever played chess or a complicated game with a machine? If so, how did you feel when it defeated you? (experience)
3. Why is Asimov more optimistic than Bradbury about the benefits of future technology? (values)
4. Is technology as much a blessing as a curse? (values)

Movie Critic

While Bradbury's vision of the future of technology is always skeptical and cautionary and even alarming, Isaac Asimov is nearly always optimistic and eager to extol its virtues. In his sequence of related stories on the history of robotics, "Robbie," the narrator, Susan Calvin who joined U.S. Robots and Mechanical Men in 2008, traces the development of robots from rather crude machines through increasing sophistication until they become virtually indistinguishable from humans in 2050. The first story, "Robbie," takes place before Susan Calvin joined U.S. Robots in 1998. She is present in the story as a teenage girl who observes people asking questions of the first talking robot that has been put on public display. Robbie is a nursemaid for 8-year-old Gloria Weston who can do all the things a human companion could do, except talk, and, he has much greater patience. As in "The Veldt," the parents, George and Grace Weston, disagree about wonders of technology—specifically Robbie's place in their daughter's development. George regards Gloria's companion as "the best darn robot money can buy" even costing him a half year's income. Grace, on the other hand, is so worried about "that terrible machine," she wants to get rid of it. She knows it cannot be healthy that Gloria prefers to play with Robbie, rather than other children. During his two years with Gloria, Robbie does not leave his charge for a moment. But Grace Weston also fears that something "might go wrong" with Robbie. After all, he is a machine and machines can and do sometimes fail. Our basic question then becomes: With whose attitude toward Robbie does Asimov want us to agree—with George's or with Grace's? Ample evidence in the story makes this a legitimate issue.

Although, the 2004 movie version of Asimov's collection of short stories, "I, Robot," was a commercial success, it failed to impress Asimov loyalists. While some critics defend it as a story in its own right, others point out that the screenplay, by Jeff Vintar and Akiva Goldsman, has but one explicit connection with Asimov's original story—the Three Laws of Robotics: (1) A robot may not injure a human being or, through inaction, allow a human being to come to harm; (2) A robot must obey orders given it by human beings except where such orders would conflict with the First Law; and (3) A robot must protect its own existence as long as such protection does not conflict with the First or Second Law. The Three Laws become the organizing principle and unifying theme for Asimov's *Foundation Trilogy*. The movie's chief departure from Asimov (whose stories are almost devoid of violence) is its action scenes involving police and crowds fighting or evading mobs of rampaging robots. "Robot as menace," is precisely the kind of story that Asimov abhorred. In contrast, Asimov's robot stories were the first to treat robots as useful creations that could have positive interactions with humans.

To decide if the movie is worth your students' time and discussion, visit the Wikipedia article at: http://en.wikipedia.org/wiki/I,_Robot_(movie)

ESSAY 1

"Sputnik: October 4, 1957"
Hannah Arendt

In 1957, an earth-born object made by man was launched into the universe, where for some weeks it circled the earth according to the same laws of gravitation that swing and keep in motion the celestial bodies—the sun, the moon, and the stars. To be sure, the man-made satellite was no moon or star, no heavenly body which could follow its circling path for a time span that to us mortals, bound by earthly time, lasts form eternity to eternity. Yet, for a time it managed to stay in the skies; it dwelt and moved in the proximity of the heavenly bodies as though it had been admitted tentatively to their sublime company.

This event, second in importance to no other, not even to the splitting of the atom, would have been greeted with unmitigated joy if it had not been for the uncomfortable military and political circumstances attending it. But, curiously enough, this joy was not triumphal; it was not pride or awe at the tremendousness of human power and mastery which filled the hearts of men, who now, when they looked up from the earth toward the skies, could behold there a thing of their own making. The immediate reaction, expressed on the spur of the moment, was relief about the first "step toward escape from men's imprisonment to the earth." And this strange statement, far from being the accidental slip of some American reporter, unwittingly echoed the extraordinary line which, more than twenty years ago, had been carved on the funeral obelisk of one of Russia's great scientists: "Mankind will not remain bound to the earth forever."

ESSAY 2

"Sputnik: October 4, 1957"
Smithsonian

On October 4, 1957, the Soviet Union launched into orbit a 184-pound sphere carrying a radio transmitter, enough batteries to run it for about two weeks, and four car-radio-style antennas, swept back to conform to the shape of the nose cone in which it rode atop its launch vehicle.

James Van Allen remembers Sputnik differently from most Americans. On a South Pacific expedition aboard the Navy's U.S.S. Glacier to study cosmic rays for the International Geophysical Year (IGY) at the time of its launch, he heard the news on the Armed Forces Radio.

"Before I swallowed it, I wanted to personally confirm it," he recalled in an interview at the Smithsonian National Air and Space Museum (NASM). The ship's radioman picked up a signal at the right frequency, and soon Van Allen and his team were listening to Sputnik's steady beeping with astonishment at the strength of the signal. Checking its orbital period, the length of the passes during which the ship's receiver held the signal, and the change in frequency of the signal as it passed like a fast-moving train, they convinced themselves that this was in fact the Russian satellite.

Sputnik demonstrated the muscle of Soviet rocketry, but the satellite was mainly for show: it carried no scientific instruments and took no measurements in space. The launch intensified a scientific and technological competition that continues to this day. The United States was close to launch itself, and had intended all along to orbit apparatus that could measure and record the space environment. Scientists like Van Allen wanted to show, as did the government, that space could be used for peaceful purposes as well as for the missiles of war.

ESSAY 3

"Sputnik: Dawn of the Space Age"
James Glieck*

It wasn't until the year 4.5 billion or so (reckoning from the birth of the planet) that an earthly life form managed to hurl some stuff into orbit—beyond the atmosphere, to permanent residence in outer space, high enough to look down and see our tiny globe for what it is.

Counted another way, it was October 4, 1957. Russians called the first satellite Sputnik, the American president decided to go golfing and just about everyone else considered the event momentous and scary. *Satellite* was a fancy word. Headline writers called these things *moons*. And why not?

Sputnik was a moon that beeped. That was its entire function, accomplished by a small radio transmitter, four antennas and a few days' worth of batteries. Plenty of scientists and rocket buffs were listening down below and hatching grander plans. Already, Arthur C. Clarke, the science-fiction writer, had performed one of the millennium's most astounding feats of invention. In 1945, he calculated and published a complete plan for using satellites to relay radio signals. Television had barely arrived, and Clarke announced satellite television—telephone, too. All in all, he imagined a communications system to unite the globe.

And so it is, a whole forty-three years later. Earth, previously naked, has acquired a glittering veil of satellites. They beam our words and pictures hither and yon, and they measure and monitor and spy on the farthest corners of our world, as they forever plunge, in their gravity-defying fashion, past the horizon. Some practically hover, geosynchronously, 23,000 miles high. Others skim past at much lower altitudes.

Here's how crowded the sky has become: the grandly and redundantly named United States Space Command Space Control Center tracks more than 8,000 nontrivial objects, ranging from functional communications satellites to lost gloves (careless astronauts!). Smaller detritus can't even be counted.

We've littered our bit of the cosmos with millions or billions of pea-size or mite-size junk fragments. There is talk of sending up robot satellites to collect the trash.

* *New York Times Magazine* (April 18, 1999).

Source Texts and
Related Readings

Adler, M. J. (1940, July 6). How to mark a book. *The Saturday Review.*

Adler, M. J. (1940). *How to read a book: The art of getting a liberal education.* New York: Simon & Schuster.

Adler, M. J. (1948). *A guide for leaders of great book discussion groups.* Chicago: Great Books Foundation.

Asimov, I. (1977). Robbie. In *I, Robot* (pp. 11-30). New York: Ballatine Books.

Barthes, R. (1975). *The pleasure of the text.* New York: Hill and Wang.

Bloom, B. (Ed.). (1956) *Taxonomy of educational objectives.* New York: McKay.

Bone, J., & Johnson, R. (1997). *Understanding the film: An introduction to film appreciation* (5th ed.) Urbana, IL: National Council of Teachers of English.

Bradbury, R. (1965). The veldt. In *The vintage Bradbury* (pp. 13-28). New York: Random House; The veldt. In *The illustrated man* (pp. 7-19). New York: Doubleday.

Bruner, J. (1960). *The process of education.* New York: Alfred A. Knopf.

Canady, R., & Rettig, M. (1999). *Teaching in the block: Strategies for engaging active learners.* Larchmont, NY: Eye on Education.

Christenbury, L., & Kelly, P. (1983). *Questioning: A path to critical thinking.* Urbana, IL: National Council of Teachers of English.

Costanzo, W. (1992). *Reading the movies: Twelve great films on video and how to teach them.* Urbana, IL: National Council of Teachers of English.

Daniels, H. (1994). *Literature circles: Voice and choice in the student-centered classroom.* York, ME: Stenhouse.

Daniels, H. (2002). *Literature circles: Voice and choice in book clubs & reading groups.* York, ME: Stenhouse.

Daniels, H., & Steineke, N. (2004). *Mini-lessons for literature circles.* Portsmouth, NH: Heinemann

DiCamillo, K. (2001). *Because of Winn Dixie.* Cambridge, MA: Candlewick Press.

Faulkner, W. (1950). Two soldiers. In *Collected Stories of William Faulkner* (pp. 81-99). New York: Random House.

Hansberry, L. (1958). *A raisin in the sun.* New York: New American Library.

Frye, N. (1970). *The educated imagination.* Bloomington: Indiana University Press.

Holt, J. (1982). *How children fail.* Reading, PA: Perseus Books.

Holt, J. (1984). *How children learn.* Reading, PA: Perseus Books.

Kutz, E., & Roskelly, H. (1991). *An unquiet pedagogy: Transforming practice in the English classroom.* Portsmouth, NH: Boynton/Cook.

Lewis, C. S. (2002). *The lion, the witch, and the wardrobe.* New York: Harper Collins.

Mann, T. (1969). *Magic mountain.* New York: Alfred A. Knopf.

McCullers, C. (1993). Sucker. In *Collected stories of Carson McCullers* (pp. 1-10). Boston: Houghton Mifflin.

Monaco, J. (2000) *How to read a film: The world of movies, media, and multimedia.* New York: Oxford University Press.

Neugeboren, J. (1965). *Best American short stories.* **New York: Farrar, Straus & Giroux.**

Orwell, G. (1954) *Animal farm.* **New York: Harcourt Brace.**

Richards, I. A. (1942). *How to read [reap] a page: A course in efficient reading.* Boston: Beacon Press.

Romano, T. (1955). *Clearing the way: Working with teenage writers.* Dallas, TX: Heinemann.

Rosenblatt, L. (1968) *Literature as exploration.* New York: Noble and Noble.

Rosenblatt, L. (1978) *The reader, the text, and the poem.* Carbondale: Southern Illinois University Press.

Ryken, L., & Mead, M. (2005). *A reader's guide through the wardrobe.* Downers Grove, IL: InterVarsity Press.

Stafford, J. (1964). *Bad characters.* **New York: Farrar, Straus; Collected Stories (1969) and (1981). Bad characters. In J. Warriner (Ed.),** *Short stories: Characters in conflict* **(pp. 260-285). New York: Harcourt Brace Jovanovich.**

Teasley, A. B., & Wilder, A. (1997). *Reel conversations: Reading films with young adults.* Portsmouth, NH: Boynton/Cook.

Tolstoy, L. (2002). *Classic tales and fables for children.* Amherst, NY: Prometheus Books.

Updike, J. (1987) Separating. **In D. Bergman & D. Epstein (Eds.),** *The Heath guide to literature* **(pp. 260-268). Lexington, MA: D C Heath and Co.**

Warren, R., & Wellek, W. (1956). *Theory of literature.* New York: Harcourt, Brace.

Whitehead, A. N. (1929). *The aims of education.* New York: Macmillan.